Kings
of
Praise

by J. Patrick Griffin, Jr.
with Carlos Aceves

The Mary Ellen Group

Unless otherwise noted, all Scriptures are taken from the Holy Bible, The New King James Version, Copyright © 1987, 1979, 1980 by Thomas Nelson Inc. Used by Permission of Thomas Nelson Publisher.

Cover Design by Hector S. Salgado, with technical assistance from Mike Miller. Graphic Artistry by Lawrence Bezuska.

ISBN 978-0-9785233-1-2
Library of Congress Catalogue Card Number: 2008911263

Dedicated to...

Amanda Marie Quintero.
The first of my wonderful nieces and
nephews, and the first of the grandchildren
born to Patrick Sr. and Mary Ellen Griffin.
So that all of you can know the
richness of life our God has provided in
Christ.

And, by Carlos,

Samantha Maxine Aceves Ortega,
my beloved daughter
and my inspiration by the
grace of God.

Table of Contents

Introduction

Introduction

Does it ever seem the days of long ago were happier? Do you wish you could retrieve the sweetness of special times from the yesterdays of your life? What if the most wonderful moments could remain in the present forever? In *Kings of Praise* you will learn how you can fill every moment with eternal value by investing that moment with joyful praise.

Jesus instructed believers to "lay up for yourselves treasures in heaven, where neither moth nor rust destroys and where thieves do not break in and steal" (Mt 6:20). Although your lifetime on this earth is quickly passing, and even the best of times are here, then gone, you can make every moment last forever by filling the moment with praise.

The Scripture refers to "the sacrifice of praise" (Jer 33:11), "the sacrifice of thanksgiving" (Ps 116:17), and the "sacrifices of joy" (Ps 27:6). Are your dreams broken? Are you burdened and cast down? By the continual sacrifice of joyful praise your life will change on the inside and on the outside.

Regardless of the circumstances, you can beautify your days with songs of praise from sun-up till sundown and all through the night. By filling your heart with praise you will fill your heart with the Spirit of God who brings us "power from on high" for a life of triumph and abundance through the name of Jesus (Eph 5:18-19; Lk 24:49; 2Cor 2:14; Jn 10:10).

The Book of First Peter identifies all believers as "a royal priesthood" commissioned and equipped "to offer up spiritual sacrifices acceptable to God through Jesus Christ" (2:9,5). As a royal priest your offerings to God are a delightful fragrance in His nostrils (Ps 50:23; 69:30-31), and the Scripture teaches us that a lifestyle of praise is the truly good life, the beautiful life. As the psalmist says:

> "Praise the Lord! For it is good to sing praises
> to our God; for it is pleasant, and praise is
> beautiful" (Ps 147:1).

You will ignite your faith and revolutionize your life by a continual offering of "spiritual sacrifices acceptable to God" in the form of praise and good works. As the Book of Hebrews summarizes in the following verses:

> "Therefore by Him let us CONTINUALLY
> offer the sacrifice of praise to God, that is, the
> fruit of our lips, giving thanks to His name.

"But do not forget to do good and to share, for with such sacrifices God is well pleased" (Heb 13:15-16).

Jesus explained, "By this My Father is glorified, that you bear much fruit" (Jn 15:8), and the fruit we bear is the priestly offering of good works and praise.

Praise is a bold expression of the faith by which all things are possible. In *Kings of Praise* you will learn from Scripture how praising God is an act of worship and a weapon of war. You will learn how the power of God will overtake your life with the fullness of His favor as you please Him continuously by the offerings of praise. By filling your heart with joyful praise your faith will mature for a godly lifetime of good works and of mighty works beyond what you had imagined, and you will march in triumph through all situations by "the power of God through faith" expressed in joyful praise.

When the people of Jerusalem broke out in praise, the opponents of Christ urged silence. But Jesus explained that "if these should keep silent, the stones would immediately cry out" (Lk 19:40). Would you let the stones praise God in your place? Would you let the rocks inherit your blessing? The sacrifice of praise is commanded by God as your continual priestly duty, and by fulfilling your duty as a priest you will experience your authority as a king.

If your life is busy and you feel frustration at having "so little time for the Lord," you will learn how you can richly please the Lord all day long on even your busiest days. Your spirit will learn to praise God the way your lungs have learned to breathe, and the joy of the Lord will spill from your heart like rivers of water for others to drink.

The Book of Acts records the baptism of an Ethiopian eunuch by the evangelist, Philip. After the baptism, "when they came up out of the water," Philip departed and the eunuch "went on his way rejoicing" (8:39). There is no reason to think he ever stopped rejoicing, and there is no reason for anyone in Christ to ever stop rejoicing. Even in the worst of times we can be "sorrowful, yet always rejoicing" (2Cor 6:10). By constant praise you will fill each moment with joy and power in the Holy Spirit, and your heart will surge with new motivation as the Lord takes control of all that concerns you.

In this book we will focus on the offering of praise as a continual act of worship and a devastating weapon of war, showing from exciting examples in the Old and New Testaments why you should commit your life to praising God day and night.

You will read about Paul and Silas shackled in a prison, and learn from their example how the chains in your own life will give way to the relentless assault of praise. You will read about Jehoshaphat, king of Judah, and learn from his example how putting praise ahead of every effort and every thought will bring you deep into the power of God that works through faith. You will read of these and other historical examples that show the life-changing relationship between joyful praise and boldness of faith. As one Christian said in a note to the authors after he'd read a study on praise taken from the book: "The (study) on praise changed my life."

1

Rejoice in His Word!

*"Then they believed His words;
they sang His praise." (Ps 106:12)*

Are your circumstances harsh and the difficulties accumulating? If so, you can triumph through God's favor by placing joyful praise ahead of everything. Rejoicing in the face of staggering problems is not a denial of the legitimacy of life's concerns (finances, health, troubled relationships, loss of a loved one); rather, it is a confession of confidence in the faithfulness of God to provide what is needed for those who come boldly. The following study will show you from Scripture how the power of God works through faith expressed in joyful praise.

When the angel Gabriel delivered God's word to Mary, saying, "you will conceive in your womb and bring forth a Son," the virgin did not waver in unbelief but said to the heavenly messenger:

> "Behold, the maidservant of the Lord! Let it be
> to me according to your word" (Lk 1:31,38).

For a virgin to bring forth a child is no less a miracle than for a dead person to rise from the grave. The Old Testament provides at least two examples of the dead rising by God's power, but no one before Mary had ever witnessed a virgin giving birth. As with Abraham and Sarah when entrusted with a remarkable promise, Mary also "did not waver at the promise of God through unbelief, but was strengthened in faith, giving glory to God, and being fully convinced that what He had promised He was also able to perform" (Rom 4:20-21).

After Mary had received the word she "went into the hill country with haste, to a city of Judah, and entered the house of Zacharias and greeted Elizabeth," who said to Mary:

> "Blessed is she who believed, for there will be
> a fulfillment of those things which were told
> her from the Lord" (Lk 1:39-40, 45).

Mary, who at that early time would have felt no physical signs of pregnancy, did not wait for physical evidence before rejoicing and praising God:

> "And Mary said: "My soul magnifies the Lord,
> and my spirit has rejoiced in God my Savior…
> henceforth all generations will call me blessed.
> For He who is mighty has done great things for

me, and holy is His name'" (vss 46-49).

Like Sarah before her, Mary needed no visible evidence before rejoicing in the word of the promise. As the Scripture testifies of Sarah:

> "By faith Sarah herself also received strength
> to conceive seed, and she bore a child when she
> was past the age, because she judged Him
> faithful who had promised" (Heb 11:11).

Both of these women received fruit in the womb when they joyfully confessed that "with God nothing will be impossible" (Lk 1:37).

Does your own life feel like an empty womb? If so, you can fill all of your emptiness by the one sure step of rejoicing in the word of God. Rather than waiting for visible evidence of blessing, remember the Scripture that tells us "the desert shall rejoice and blossom as the rose" (Isa 35:1). The natural mind is conditioned to wait for the blossom before having joy, but the mind of faith boldly rejoices when the season is still dry. As Jesus testified of Abraham, who was promised a Son whom he saw only through the eye of faith:

> "Your father Abraham rejoiced to see My day,
> and he saw it and was glad" (Jn 8:56).

Jesus, whom the Scripture identifies as "the Son of Abraham" (Mt 1:1), was born about eighteen centuries after the word of the promise was given. But Abraham rejoiced so completely in the word that he enjoyed the day of Christ while living eighteen centuries before His birth.

For Abraham and Sarah, as with Mary after them, the rejoicing of faith preceded the blossom of the desert, and all these things "were written for our learning" (Rom 15:4).

However dry or threatening your life-situation may seem, these Biblical examples and exhortations were written for your encouragement and wisdom in the faith. Do not underestimate the relevance of these examples to your own life. "All things are possible to him who believes" (Mk 9:23), and by constant rejoicing in the word of the Lord you will purify your heart from the doubt that hinders "the power of God through faith" (1Pet 1:5). The Lord is "able to do exceedingly abundantly above all that we ask or think" (Eph 3:20), and even the threat of death becomes a slave to the welfare of those who rejoice with confidence in the word of the living God.

When the prophet Jeremiah was hunted by "the men of Anathoth" who had devised a scheme to "cut him off from the land of the living," the prophet cried out to God and asked:

"Why does the way of the wicked prosper?" (Jer 11:19,21; 12:1).

The Lord acknowledged to Jeremiah that those who wrongly persecuted him "have dealt treacherously with you; yes, they have called a multitude after you" (12:6). But the situation did not improve for the complaining man of God, who later said:

"Woe is me, my mother, that you have borne
me, a man of strife and a man of contention to
the whole earth!" (15:10a).

It seemed to Jeremiah that the whole world was pressing against him, and that "every one of them curses me" (15:10b). Do you know this feeling? Does it seem that nothing is working the way it should and your life is an impossible burden? Is your neighborhood flooded with gang and criminal activity, and do you fear for your children's vulnerability to the corrupting influences? If any of these are a threat to you, you can flee to the remedy that Jeremiah found when surrounded by hatred and violence:

"Your words were found, and I ate them, and
Your word was to me the joy and rejoicing of
my heart; for I am called by Your name, O
Lord God of hosts" (15:16).

By rejoicing in the Lord's word we wrap our lives into His name, and there is no greater way to call on His name than to rejoice in His word. As the Scripture tells us in the Psalms:

"You have magnified Your word above all
Your name" (138:2).

By rejoicing in His word we come to the refuge of His name:

"You are my hiding place and my shield; I hope in Your word" (Ps 119:114).

The Scripture tells us "the word of God is living and powerful" (Heb 4:12), and that man shall live "by every word of God" (Lk 4:4). Only the mind of faith can sink its teeth into the word and drink its power, and nothing is impossible for those who believe without doubting.

There is a faith that merely gets by, but if you want the faith that moves mountains you will say with the psalmist:

"I rejoice at Your word as one who finds great treasure" (Ps 119:162).

When a person finds a great treasure, his heart leaps with excitement and he thinks of the ways this treasure will change his life. According to Jesus, "If you have faith and do not doubt", your life will change so dramatically that "nothing will be impossible for you" (Mt 21:21; 17:20). To fully experience the treasure of God's word, all we need is a drop of pure faith:

"(I)f you have faith as a mustard seed, you will say to this mountain, 'Move from here to there,' and it will move; and nothing will be impossible for you" (Mt 17:20).

Is your heart afflicted by the impurities of doubt? Is unbelief hindering your experience of the living power of

Rejoice in His Word!

God's word? The remedy for a doubting heart is to rejoice with constant praise in the treasure of the word. As the psalmist confessed in another place:

> "Your testimonies...are the rejoicing of my heart" (Ps 119:111).

> "I have rejoiced in the way of Your testimonies, as much as in all riches" (Ps 119:14).

"The word of the Lord is proven" (Ps 18:30), and we should boldly rejoice in the unshakable certainty of His "exceedingly great and precious promises" (2Pet 1:4). The Lord has given us a treasure that will transform our lives and empower us to walk on water if needed, but this treasure remains largely untapped until we seize the word with aggressive rejoicing that annihilates doubt.

Those who have the faith that moves mountains do not wring their hands and mumble their confession like a whimpering sigh. Even in the worst of times an aggressive believer will "rejoice before You according to the joy of harvest, as men rejoice when they divide the spoil" (Isa 9:3). The visible world can intimidate the natural eye, but the rejoicing believer stands in awe of God's word:

> "Princes persecute me without a cause, but my heart stands in awe of Your word" (Ps 119:161).

The word of God, which brought the universe into existence and holds it together, is "living and powerful" and worthy of our joyful confidence. As David confessed in a song after his enemies had captured him:

> "Whenever I am afraid, I will trust in You. In God (I will praise His word), in God I have put my trust; I will not fear. What can flesh do to me?" (Ps 56:3-4)

We note that David did not sing this song from a place of physical safety and comfort. The Philistines had "captured him in Gath," but David filled his heart with the treasure of God's word and left no room in his thoughts for the cancer of doubt.

The Biblical history of David's life shows a man who triumphed through joy. In his many adversities, and sometimes against staggering odds, he "strengthened himself in the Lord his God" by offering songs of praise (cf. 1Sam 30:6; Ps 56:13; 27:1). For seventeen years he ran for his life, hiding in caves and wandering through deserts, all the while composing psalms expressing his joyful confidence in the mercy and faithfulness of God. By songs of joyful praise David fixed his mind on the Lord, providing us with a living example of the Scripture that tells us "You will keep him in perfect peace, whose mind is stayed on You" (Isa 26:3).

Faith and rejoicing link profoundly in the Scriptures, as in the following verse:

"But let all those rejoice who put their trust in
You; let them ever shout for joy" (Ps 5:11a).

Faith without rejoicing is common, but this is not a
Biblical faith. As David tells us again in another Psalm:

"For our heart shall rejoice in Him, because we
have trusted in His holy name" (33:21).

But where there is no rejoicing our faith will limp and
stagger.

A failure to rejoice places a person
outside the will of God, as the Scripture
makes clear in the following passage:

"Rejoice always, pray without ceasing, in everything give thanks; for
this [continuous prayer with joyful
thanksgiving] is the will of God in
Christ Jesus for you" (1Thess 5:16-
18).

> *This treasure
> remains
> largely
> untapped
> until we seize
> the Word with
> aggressive
> rejoicing that
> annihilates
> doubt.*

By continual rejoicing we abide in
the Lord's will and set fire to faith for the
burning away of doubt.

When Paul drew near to Jerusalem for the last time,
knowing that "chains and tribulations" awaited him, he spoke
to the Christians about his resolve to "finish my race with
joy" (Acts 20:22-24). Without the fuel of joy our faith will

struggle to endure, so the apostle exhorts us again and again to "rejoice in the Lord always" (Phil 4:4). The book of Hebrews was written to Christians enduring harsh and prolonged affliction, and the Scripture exhorts them to "hold fast the confidence and the rejoicing of the hope firm to the end" (Heb 3:6). These Christians "joyfully accepted the plundering of (their) goods," and they were assured that by steadfast rejoicing "firm to the end" they would "imitate those who through faith and patience inherit the promises" (10:34; 6:12).

> *Our joyfulness expresses adoration, gratitude, and confidence in Christ as our Shepherd and King.*

Our joyfulness expresses adoration, gratitude, and confidence in Christ as our Shepherd and King. This joyfulness is not dependent on circumstance, as Paul testified in a letter written from a prison cell in Rome:

"I thank my God…always in every prayer of mine making request for you all with joy…I shall remain and continue with you all for your progress and joy of faith …I am glad and rejoice with you all…Finally, my brethren, rejoice in the Lord… rejoice in Christ Jesus. Rejoice in the Lord always. Again I will say, rejoice!" (Phil 1:3-4, 25; 2:17; 3:1; 4:4).

From his vile circumstance he magnified God with continual rejoicing, testifying that "I have learned in whatever state

Rejoice in His Word!

I am, to be content" (4:11). If we aim for the triumph that Paul experienced, we will rejoice as Paul rejoiced. As he said to us all by the authority of the Spirit: "I urge you, imitate me" (1Cor 4:16).

Whatever is going on in your life, you can seize the upper hand by an instant, one-step leap into a lifestyle of aggressive praise with joyful thanksgiving. You can do this at all times. You can do this in all situations. You can do this right now.

We know from Scripture that "the word of the Lord is proven," but the Scripture also tells us:

"If you will not believe, surely you shall not be established" (Isa 7:9).

How do we deal with unbelief? We vaporize it with joy. As the prophet Habakkuk also confessed, in a song recorded for our learning:

"Though the fig tree may not blossom, nor fruit be on the vines; though the labor of the olive may fail, and the fields yield no food; though the flock may be cut off from the fold, and there be no herd in the stalls—yet I will rejoice in the Lord, I will joy in the God of my salvation. The Lord God is my strength; He will make my feet like deer's feet, and He will make me walk on my high hills" (Hab 3:17-19).

13

By rejoicing in the Lord's strength we walk in His strength, and we can do this when the cupboards are empty and the bank account dry. Regardless of the severity of our circumstances, and regardless of what threatens us, the Scripture commands us to cast our burden on the Lord by joyfully giving praise at all times:

> "Rejoice in the Lord always...Be anxious for nothing" (Phil 4:4,6).

These two sayings connect. We cannot have the one without the other. By aggressive, continuous rejoicing in the word of the Lord no room is left in the heart for the burden of anxiety.

By joyfully giving praise we give the Lord our burden, and every new burden becomes an immediate cause for rejoicing in a new opportunity for God to show Himself faithful. With so much Scriptural exhortation, and with so many Biblical examples, we should not hesitate to cast our burden on the Lord by rejoicing in the treasure of His word. "Has He said, and will He not do? Or has He spoken, and will He not make it good?" (Num 23:19). In the flesh we may feel weak and insufficient, but the Scripture assures us from beginning to end that by rejoicing in His word we will triumph through the favor of His name.

2

Praise God!

*"Therefore by Him let us continually
offer the sacrifice of praise to God." (Heb 13:15a)*

Whatever your situation, whatever the odds against you or the severity of the threat, God has provided a tested and proven advantage. Praise is identified in Scripture as a weapon of warfare guaranteed to defeat what opposes the glory of God in your life. The Scripture in Psalms speaks of how believers will "triumph in Your praise" (106:47), and the following study will show you from Scripture how praising God is the proven way to experience the Lord's power for triumph in every situation.

Praise is identified in Scripture as an offering of worship and a weapon of war:

"Whoever offers praise glorifies Me" (Ps

50:23).

"From the lips of children and infants You have ordained praise because of your enemies, to silence the foe and the avenger" (Ps 8:2, NIV: cf. Mt 21:16).

Are your circumstances harsh and the difficulties accumulating? If so, you can triumph through God's favor by placing the weapon of joyful praise ahead of everything. Without leaving other things undone, rejoice in the faithfulness of God by putting praise ahead of every effort, every prayer, every thought. The Bible is loaded with exhortations and historical examples of God's power working through the praise of His people, and we have no reason for doubting His involvement through our praises today.

Six centuries before the birth of Jesus, when Jehoshaphat reigned as king over Judah, an assembly of Gentile armies invaded the homeland of God's people. The Book of Second Chronicles records how "the people of Moab with the people of Ammon, and others with them besides the Ammonites, came to battle against Jehoshaphat. Then some came and told Jehoshaphat, saying, "A great multitude is coming against you"" (20:1-2). The passage records that "Jehoshaphat feared, and set himself to seek the Lord" (vs 3). After the king had assembled his people in Jerusalem, he prayed aloud in the temple court:

"O Lord God...we have no power against this

great multitude that is coming against us; nor
do we know what to do, but our eyes are upon
You" (vss 6,12).

In reading this Biblical history we should not remain
bystanders passively watching. We want to enter spiritually into
the situation and learn for ourselves a lesson in the art of war
against great opposition. Who among us, believers in Christ on
the earth today, can fail to identify with the feeling expressed
by Jehoshaphat in his impossible situation? In times of great
distress, when the difficulties accumulate and we feel overwhelmed by all that comes against us, we can say with Jehoshaphat in our prayer to God: I have no power against all that is
coming against me, nor do I have the wisdom to know what to
do.

But in our helplessness we can glorify God by fighting
with the weapon used by Jehoshaphat:

> "And when he had consulted with the people,
> he appointed those who should sing to the
> Lord, and who should praise the beauty of holi-
> ness, as they went out before the army and
> were saying: "Praise the Lord, for His mercy
> endures forever"" (vs 21).

With no strength or wisdom of his own, the king placed
all his care in the hand of God by concentrating on praise. The
next verse shows us what happens when the Lord's people put
praise ahead of everything:

"Now when they began to sing and to praise, the Lord set ambushes against the people of Ammon, Moab, and Mount Seir, who had come against Judah; and they were defeated."

By placing praise ahead of every concern, the people of Judah laid hold on "the power of God through faith" for deliverance and triumph against impossible odds.

The Scripture tells us that God has "ordained praise... to silence the foe." We know that God is faithful to His word, and we know He is "the same yesterday, today, and forever" (Heb 13:8). If He acted through the praise of His people yesterday, why should we think He will fail to act through the praise of His people today? The Scripture says we will "triumph in Your praise," and whoever lives for God's praise through faith in the Son is guaranteed the triumph at all times in all situations. As the Scripture assures us again in Second Corinthians:

"Now thanks be to God who always leads us in triumph in Christ" (2:14).

And again in First Corinthians:

"But thanks be to God, who gives us the victory through our Lord Jesus Christ" (15:57).

We have read the account of the Lord's intervention through the praise of His people in the days of Jehoshaphat, and we can use our imagination to see the singers marching before the army, marching to the battle with the voice of praise as their weapon of choice. The Scripture in Romans tells us that "whatever things were written before were written for our learning" (15:4), and what we learn from Jehoshaphat is that those who commit their lives to praising God will triumph through the power of His name.

Knowing this, shouldn't we heed the word that tells us to "continually offer the sacrifice of praise to God"?

Help is promised in time of need for those who come to God boldly: "Let us therefore come boldly to the throne of grace, that we may obtain mercy and find grace to help in time of need" (Heb 4:16). In times of need, those who come with joyful praise show the boldness of faith that lays hold on the promise and doesn't let go.

Another example of spiritual boldness is David's attitude of praise while running for his life in the Judean wilderness. David spent seventeen years in his wanderings, rejoicing through laughter and tears, singing to God in the darkest hour and saying:

"You number my wanderings; put my tears into Your bottle; are they not in Your book? When I cry out to You, then my enemies will turn back; this I know, because God is for me. In God (I will praise His word), in the Lord (I will praise His word), in God I have put my trust; I will not be afraid. What can man do to me?" (Ps 56:8-11).

David wrote this Psalm after he'd been captured by the enemy Philistines while running for his life from Saul. Rather than yielding to doubt and voicing complaints in unbelief, he offered songs of praise to boldly confess his confidence in God. David did not deny his pain or the dreadful opposition surrounding him, yet by mingling his tears with joyful praise he obtained the help that God has promised to those who come boldly.

If the Scriptures clearly establish praise as a means of triumph by God's power in Christ, why should we hesitate to praise Him continuously in even our toughest situations?

For those who walk by faith, the major enemy is doubt. The Lord Jesus, after He had caused a fig tree to wither, said:

> "Assuredly, I say to you, if you have faith and do not doubt, you will not only do what was done to the fig tree, but also if you say to this mountain, 'Be removed and be cast into the sea,' it will be done. And whatever things you ask in prayer, believing, you will receive" (Mt 21:21-22).

This remarkable saying shows that nothing is impossible for those who "have faith and do not doubt." But how do we drive from our minds the doubt that hinders our experience of God's power and the fullness of His favor?

When the apostles said to the Lord, "Increase our faith," Jesus answered: "If you have faith as a mustard seed, you can say to this mulberry tree, 'Be pulled up by the roots

20

and be planted in the sea,' and it would obey you…and nothing will be impossible for you" (Lk 17:5-6; Mt 17:20). What we need is not necessarily an increase of faith. What we need is a faith that is pure. We need a heart from which all doubt has been purged, and according to the Scripture in Psalm 8:2 the chatter of doubt is silenced by the weapon of praise: "You have ordained praise…to silence the foe."

It would seem impossible to doubt and to praise God at the same time. Praise is a high act of faith, and by continual praise we drive from our hearts the doubt that hinders our experience of God.

David, on another occasion during his wilderness wanderings, composed the sixty-third Psalm, singing:

> "Because Your lovingkindness is better than life, my lips shall praise You. Thus I will bless You while I live; I will lift up my hands in Your name…and my mouth shall praise You with joyful lips…Because You have been my help, therefore in the shadow of Your wings I will rejoice" (vss 3-5,7).

David vowed to joyfully praise the name of the Lord "while I live." His offering of praise was a way of life rather than a part-time hobby. In this Psalm he spoke of "those who seek my life, to destroy it" (vs 9). But rather than murmuring with doubt, he rejoiced with confidence, laying hold on God's power by feeding his faith with joy.

Are there people aiming to destroy something valuable

in your life? Do the odds against you seem overwhelming and unfair? If so, remember that "the word of the Lord is proven," and His word to you is:

> "Call upon Me in the day of trouble; I will deliver you, and you shall glorify Me" (Ps 50:15).

If the promise of God is that He will deliver us and we shall glorify Him, then we should jump right out and get started by glorifying Him with praise. "Whoever offers praise glorifies Me," and we should do this already no matter what the circumstance or the severity of the threat. Why should we wait to rejoice with praise when we already have the assurance of God?

> *Where there is little joy there is also little faith.*

Another example of spiritual boldness is Paul's response to the "chains and tribulations" that awaited him. Meeting with the elders of the church in Ephesus, en route to Jerusalem where great opposition had formed against him, he said:

> "I go bound in the spirit to Jerusalem, not knowing the things that will happen to me there, except that the Holy Spirit testifies in every city, saying that chains and tribulations await me. But none of these things move me; nor do I count my life dear to myself, so that I may finish my race with joy" (Acts 20:22-24a).

In the long race for the prize of glory our faith endures by feeding on joy. But where there is little joy there is also little faith.

"All things are possible to him who believes" (Mk 9:23), and there is no greater show of faith than to concentrate on praising God in a situation beyond our strength and understanding. Praise is a weapon that God has ordained to silence the foe, and a believer should use this weapon relentlessly in all situations. When Paul and Silas were beaten and chained in a prison they relied on God through joyful praise in the name of Jesus:

> "Then the multitude rose up together against [Paul and Silas]; and…when they had laid many stripes on them, they threw them into prison…and fastened their feet in the stocks. But at midnight Paul and Silas were praying and singing hymns to God, and the prisoners were listening to them. Suddenly there was a great earthquake, so that the foundations of the prison were shaken; and immediately all the doors were opened and everyone's chains were loosed" (Acts 16:22-26).

In your midnight hour you too can seize the advantage with joyful songs of praise, crushing the doubt that would otherwise hinder "the power of God through faith." The shackles and chains oppressing you are not invulnerable; they cannot resist the power of God working through faith expressed in praise. When fear and doubt, depression or anxiety, rise in your heart, answer with joyful praise and stay on the offensive. Do not underestimate the Biblical examples. God did not record these events for the purpose of literature. And remember that David reached the throne of Israel after seventeen years of "hold(ing) fast the confidence and the rejoicing of the hope firm to the end."

3

Praise Him Always!

"While I live I will praise the Lord." (Ps 146:2)

Do you ever struggle with feelings of spiritual insignificance? This is a painful problem for many Christians who truly love the Lord but do not feel valuable to God's kingdom. There are Christians who routinely spend hours in self-indulgence through television or other non-edifying entertainments, not because their desire to serve Christ is lacking, but rather because they do not believe they can bring a meaningful contribution to the work of the kingdom. The remedy for spiritual discouragement is knowing the place of praise in everyday spiritual triumph.

By offering praise we declare that we are the people of God:

"This people I have formed for Myself, they shall declare My praise" (Isa 43:21).

25

"But you [who come to God through Christ]
are…His own special people, that you may
proclaim the praises of Him who called you out
of darkness into His marvelous light; who once
were not a people but are now the people of
God" (1Pet 2:9-10a).

By proclaiming His praise we position ourselves aggressively in the ministry of God's people, and by continuing in
praise the fruitfulness of our spiritual lives increases dramatically.

The following verses confirm the link between praise
and increase:

"Let the peoples praise You, O God; let all the
peoples praise You. Then the earth shall yield
her increase; God, our own God, shall bless
us" (Ps 67:5-6).

Is your life afflicted with scarcity? If so, start praising
God and watch what happens. The Scripture tells us "the desert
shall rejoice and blossom as the rose" (Isa 35:1), and in this
verse we note how the praise of rejoicing precedes the blossom.
If your life feels like a desert, rejoice in Christ all day long and
your desert will sprout and bloom and spill over with fruit.

By abiding in joyful praise we walk in the wisdom of
those who triumph through the name of the Lord, but the unbelieving world grows ever more foolish through its refusal to
glorify heaven's King with praise and thanksgiving:

"For since the creation of the world...they are without excuse, because, although they knew God, they did not glorify [praise] Him as God, nor were thankful, but became futile in their thoughts, and their foolish hearts were darkened" (Rom 1:20-21).

Denying the Lord praise leads to futile thinking and darkness of heart. Denying Him praise identifies a person with the unbelieving world, but through a lifestyle of praise we set our minds on things above to embrace the customs of heaven.

Our Lord Jesus Christ prayed: "Our Father in heaven... Your will be done on earth as it is in heaven" (Mt 6:9-10). In heaven they are always praising God:

"And they do not rest day or night, saying: "Holy, holy, holy, Lord God Almighty, who was and is and is to come!"" (Rev 4:8b).

If this is what they are always doing in heaven, this is what we should always be doing on earth. By praising God we breathe the culture and the atmosphere of heaven, and we fulfill the Scripture that tells us to "set your mind on things above, not on things on the earth" (Col 3:2). In times of distress we can lean on our own understanding and focus on the power of what rises against us, or we can walk on the stormy water by fixing our minds on Jesus with steadfast songs of praise.

The Scripture in Isaiah tells us, "You will keep him in perfect peace, whose mind is stayed on You" (26:3), and there is no better way to fix our minds on Jesus than to ceaselessly offer the sacrifice of praise.

The Scripture tells us that God is "a rewarder of those who diligently seek Him" (Heb 11:6), and "those who seek Him will praise the Lord" (Ps 22:26). If we are not praising God then we are not truly seeking, and if we are seeking Him we will not stop praising.

The Scriptures repeatedly emphasize how those who seek the Lord must do so with constant and whole-hearted praise:

"Glory in His holy name; let the hearts of those rejoice who seek the Lord" (1Chron 16:10).

"Let all those who seek You rejoice and be glad in You" (Ps 40:16).

"I will praise the Lord with my whole heart" (Ps 111:1).

"I will bless the Lord at all times; His praise shall continually be in my mouth" (Ps 34:1).

"I will sing to the Lord as long as I live; I will sing praise to my God while I have my being" (Ps 104:33).

"Bless the Lord, O my soul; and all that is within me, bless His holy name!" (Ps 103:1).

"Let my mouth be filled with Your praise and
with Your glory all the day" (Ps 71:8).

When adversities storm against us, and the pain of
helplessness overwhelms us, we show our boldness of faith by
saying with the psalmist:

"I will hope continually, and will praise You
yet more and more. My mouth shall tell of
Your righteousness and Your salvation all the day, for I do not know
their limits" (Ps 71:14-15).

> *If He can bring a child from a virgin who believed, why set a limit on what He will accomplish through the boldness of your joyful faith today?*

By constantly praising God we
show a faith that sets no limits on what He
will accomplish. As Gabriel said to the rejoicing virgin: "For with God nothing will
be impossible" (Lk 1:37). If He can bring a
child from a virgin who believed, why set a
limit on what He will accomplish through
the boldness of your joyful faith today?
When the Israelites lifted their voice in
praise to God the walls of Jericho fell
(Joshua 6:20), and "whatever things were
written before were written for our learn-
ing." We learn from Jericho and from other Biblical examples
that "the weapons of our warfare are...mighty in God for pulling down strongholds" (2Cor 10:4). Whatever adversities and
threats are coming against you, there is no opposition equal to

the power of God working through faith expressed in joyful praise. No matter what your circumstances, you can say with Hannah the mother of Samuel: "I smile at my enemies, because I rejoice in Your salvation" (1Sam 2:1).

By praising God you will lay hold of His strength: "The Lord is my strength and song" (Ps 118:14). But without the song there is no strength, so the Scripture tells us again: "Sing aloud to God our strength" (Ps 81:1). The Apostle Paul constantly, at all times and in all situations, offered to God the sacrifice of praise through Jesus Christ, and because of this he could boldly say: "I can do all things through Christ who strengthens me" (Phil 4:13). As David in the wilderness also testified with joyful song: "For by You I can run against a troop, by my God I can leap over a wall" (Ps 18:29).

If your life is afflicted by a wall of opposition you can make the leap by shouting to God with joyful praise.

"Oh, clap your hands, all you peoples! Shout to God with the voice of triumph!" (Ps 47:1).

"Shout joyfully to the Lord, all the earth; break forth in song, rejoice, and sing praises" (Ps 98:4).

If a troop of adversity comes against you, you can boldly say with the psalmist: "Though an army may encamp against me, my heart shall not fear; though war may rise against me, in this I will be confident" (27:3).

When the rebellious tribes of Israel came to fight

against the house of David which reigned over the kingdom of Judah, the army of Judah found itself caught in a pincer-movement with no way of escape:

> "Jeroboam [king of the breakaway tribes of Israel] caused an ambush to go around behind them; so they were in front of Judah, and the ambush was behind them. And when Judah looked around, to their surprise the battle line was at both front and rear" (2Chron 13:13-14a).

Outmaneuvered by their opponents and facing almost certain defeat, the men of Judah "cried out to the Lord, and the priests sounded the trumpets. Then the men of Judah gave a shout; and as the men of Judah shouted, it happened that God struck Jeroboam and all Israel...And the children of Israel fled before Judah, and God delivered them into their hand" (vss 14b-16).

Do you feel ambushed "at both the front and the rear"? Do you see opposition staring down from strong positions? Whatever your difficulty or the strength of the odds against you, you too can "shout to God with the voice of triumph" and boldly rejoice in "the victory through our Lord Jesus Christ" (Ps 47:1; 1Cor 15:57).

By constant rejoicing in the name of Christ all doubt is put to silence so that "we may boldly say: "The Lord is my helper; I will not fear. What can man do to me?"" (Heb 13:6).

By praising God we flee to His name, and whoever

would call on the Father through Christ must do so with praise:

"Praise the Lord, call upon His name" (Isa 12:4).

"According to Your name, O God, so is Your praise to the ends of the earth" (Ps 48:10).

By praising His name we walk in triumph:

"(T)o give thanks to Your holy name, to triumph in Your praise" (Ps 106:47).

By calling on Him with the voice of praise we come to His name in truth. And, "The Lord is near to all who call upon Him, to all who call upon Him in truth" (Ps 145:18).

> *By offering praise He fills our voice with the authority of His throne.*

By offering praise He fills our voice with the authority of His throne: "You are holy, enthroned in the praises of Israel" (Ps 22:3). All who come to God through Christ are authorized to offer these praises: "Rejoice, O Gentiles, with His people...Praise the Lord, all you Gentiles! Laud Him, all you peoples!" (Deut 32:43; Ps. 117:1). The great mystery of the Gospel is that Christ has united all believers, regardless of race or nationality, into one body of sonship.

"For you are all sons of God through faith in Christ Jesus...that the Gentiles should be fellow heirs [with believing Jews], of the same body, and partakers of His promise in Christ through the gospel" (Gal 3:26; Eph 3:6).

Through faith in Jesus we lift up our voice with the praise in which God sits enthroned. Knowing this, we should boldly seize the word which tells us to "be filled with the Spirit, speaking to one another in psalms and hymns and spiritual songs, singing and making melody in your heart to the Lord" (Eph 5:18b-19). In these verses we understand that by filling our hearts with songs of praise we have filled our hearts with the Spirit of God.

The Scripture teaches us that the Lord acts through the praise of His people:

"When I cry out to You, then my enemies will turn back; this I know, because God is for me. In God (I will praise His word), in the Lord (I will praise His word), in God I have put my trust" (Ps 56:9-11a).

"God has gone up [He acts!] with a shout, the Lord with the sound of a trumpet. Sing praises to God, sing praises! Sing praises to our King, sing praises!" (Ps 47:5-6).

If you have no trumpet to blow, slap your hand on the

33

table and shout to God in triumph! Acknowledge Him with joyful noises, remembering the Scripture which tells us, "Blessed are the people who know the joyful sound!" (Ps 89:15). Regardless of your circumstance or the threats to your success, show your confidence in the Lord by singing to Him with joy, knowing that those who commit their lives to praising God will not be denied the power of His favor.

We show our trust in the Father through Jesus by calling on Him with praise:

> "I will call upon the Lord, who is worthy to be praised; so shall I be saved from my enemies" (2Sam 22:4).

The Book of Judges records for our learning how the Lord worked with power through the praise of His people when the homeland of Israel came under attack in the days of Gideon:

> "Then all the Midianites and Amalekites, the people of the East, gathered together; and they crossed over and encamped in the Valley of Jezreel" (6:33).

The combined force of the enemy was too great for numbering:

> "[They] were lying in the valley as numerous as locusts; and their camels were without number, as the sand by the seashore in multi-

tude" (7:12).

Gideon went up against this force with only three hundred of his men, and the outnumbered Israelites brought swords to the battle but they did not rely on these:

> "Then [Gideon] divided the three hundred men into three companies, and he put a trumpet into every man's hand, with empty pitchers, and torches inside the pitchers…[They] came to the outpost of the camp at the beginning of the middle watch…Then the three companies blew the trumpets and broke the pitchers…and they cried, "The sword of the Lord and of Gideon!" And every [Israelite] man stood in his place all around the camp and the whole army ran and cried out and fled" (7:16, 19-21).

As in the days of Jehoshaphat, so also in the days of Gideon, when the people of God advanced with the weapon of praise the enemies fell back in confusion:

> "When the three hundred blew the trumpets, the Lord set every man's sword against his companion throughout the whole camp; and the army fled" (7:22a).

The Lord delights to manifest His power through praise, and with such an abundance of Biblical testimony how can we justify doubt? As the Scripture tells us in Isaiah: "If you will not believe, surely you shall not be established" (7:9). Even in the most complicated and difficult times you can establish your authority as a royal priest in Christ by putting praise ahead of everything else that you do.

The Scripture in Ephesians tells us:

"Therefore take up the whole armor of God,
that you may be able to withstand in the evil
day, and having done all, to stand" (6:13).

Only by constant praise can any of us say we have "done all." We do not put confidence in the praise itself, but rather in the power of God who works through faith expressed in praise. Nor should we think that praise is a magic formula; it is simply the wonderful means our God has ordained for us to experience His power for deliverance and triumph to the increase of His glory.

> *We do not put confidence in the praise itself, but rather in the power of God who works through faith expressed in praise.*

By proclaiming His praise we declare that we are His people and that we live always under "the favor You have toward Your people...the benefit of Your chosen ones" (Ps 106:4-5).

Although our battles could seem to be against flesh and blood, the Scripture repeatedly assures us that "Heaven rules" (Dan 4:26). By constantly praising God we join the chorus of heaven and whatever comes against us comes also against the power and dominion of heaven's King.

By a lifestyle of praise we bring to God through Christ a continual offering of sweet-smelling aroma, and by constantly praising God we fill our hearts with His Spirit for an increase of fruitfulness and triumph in all situations.

Whatever confronts you in the present hour, whether it be fierce opposition outside of you or spiritual dryness within you, answer with praise and stay on the offensive, knowing from Scripture that you can only be defeated when you stop praising God.

4

Cling To Him In Praise!

"I will hope continually, and will praise You yet more and more." (Ps 71:14)

Do you feel that your spiritual life is less fruitful than it should be? Having believed on Jesus as Christ and Lord, are you disappointed with your growth in godliness? Are you discouraged by the burden of so many problems?

If your current circumstances are troubling, or if your spiritual life seems dry and inconsistent, you can seize "the power of God through faith" by filling your heart with praise. By constant praise you will enter into new opportunities for contributing to the work of the kingdom, and you will experience a refreshing increase of spiritual empowerment for fruitful labors and everyday godliness.

The Scripture links the meaning of life with praise, teaching us that our offerings to God are the true pleasure and value of being alive:

> "Let my soul live, and it shall praise You" (Ps 119:175).

> "Because Your lovingkindness is better than life, my lips shall praise You. Thus I will bless You while I live; I will lift up my hands in Your name" (Ps 63:3-4).

Those of us pushing up in years are sometimes amazed at how quickly a lifetime can pass. Seasons of happiness delight us while they last, and we do our best to relish the beauty of each moment but the moment slips away and never comes back. Poets speak often of "the days of the lost sunshine," and the Scripture also refers to how quickly "the grass withers, the flower fades." The earth spins, and we all know the yearning for good things lost to the curse of time. But through Jesus our Lord we have power to "redeem the time" and possess each moment forever.

> "The grass withers, the flower fades, but the word of our God stands forever" (Isa 40:8).

If the word of the Lord stands forever, then by all means we should invest every moment in the word. And the word of the Lord tells us:

> "Whoever offers praise glorifies Me" (Ps 50:23a).

Cling To Him In Praise!

Time that is used for self-indulgence is lost to the past and cannot be retrieved, but a moment invested in the Father's glory is a moment that lives forever in the kingdom of God. It is a moment stored up "in heaven, where neither moth nor rust destroys and where thieves do not break in and steal" (Mt 6:20). When the Lord extended Hezekiah's life, the king measured the value of his years by the opportunity those years would provide for bringing glory to God:

> "For Sheol cannot thank You, Death cannot praise You...The living, the living man, he shall praise You, as I do this day" (Isa 38:18-19a).

As citizens of the kingdom we measure life's value by the opportunity it provides for bringing glory to God, and we can glorify Him with praise at all times in all situations:

> "While I live I will praise the Lord; I will sing praises to my God while I have my being" (Ps 146:2).

> "Therefore by (Christ) let us continually offer the sacrifice of praise to God, that is, the fruit of our lips, giving thanks to His name" (Heb 13:15).

We should praise the Father through Jesus—not sometimes, and not most of the time. We should praise the Lord as often as we breathe. For those who come to God through Christ, joyful praise is spiritual breathing. "Let everything that has breath praise the Lord" (Ps 150:6). But when we are not praising God we are spiritually suffocating.

Jesus explained: "By this My Father is glorified, that you bear much fruit" (Jn 15:8). This compares with: "Whoever offers praise glorifies Me." Every moment of life is opportunity to glorify God with the fruit of praise, "speaking to one another in psalms and hymns and spiritual songs, singing and making melody in your heart to the Lord, giving thanks always for all things to God the Father in the name of our Lord Jesus Christ" (Eph 5:19-20).

We should praise Him with our deeds, our words, our thoughts, and we should use the imagination of our hearts to devise new ways of joyfully praising Him. By a lifestyle of praise we lay hold of the fullness our Lord came to give, and the spiritual value of praise could not possibly be overestimated.

As a general rule, and whenever possible, what should the people of God be talking about?

"They shall speak of the glory of Your kingdom, and talk of Your power" (Ps 145:11).

"Sing to Him, sing psalms to Him; talk of all His wondrous works! Glory in His holy name" (Ps 105:2-3a).

If you seriously desire a more fruitful spiritual life,

spend as much time as possible with people who habitually celebrate the kingdom of God in their conversation. The Scripture tells us the Lord listens with delight to the conversation of those who speak to one another of His goodness and glory:

> "Then those who feared the Lord spoke to one another, and the Lord listened and heard them; so a book of remembrance was written before Him for those who fear the Lord and who meditate on His name" (Mal 3:16).

We should not underestimate the compromising effect of worldly conversation. This is a terrible plague that weakens the faith of many believers, and whatever weakens faith also weakens our experience of the Lord's power in our lives. Worldly conversation is not necessarily vulgar, but it does not edify, and whatever does not edify is of no value to God's kingdom or to His glory among men.

The power and wisdom of godly conversation is emphasized throughout Scripture, and we are told that "whatever you do in word or deed, do all in the name of the Lord Jesus" (Col 3:17). The entire stream of our conversation should be an offering to God through Christ, as Paul tells us again in Colossians:

> "Let your speech always be with grace, seasoned with salt...teaching and admonishing one another in psalms and hymns and spiritual songs" (4:6; 3:16).

43

The Scripture speaks of "redeeming the time" (Col 4:5), and we should be jealous for the Lord's glory with every moment.

If we are serious in our aim to more richly experience the fullness of life that Christ came to give, we will fill our hearts with constant praise that spills over in the general flow of our speech:

> "I will also meditate on all Your work, and talk of Your deeds" (Ps 77:12).

> "My mouth shall tell of Your righteousness and Your salvation all the day...Let my mouth be filled with Your praise and with Your glory all the day...My tongue also shall talk of Your righteousness all the day long" (Ps 71:15,8,24).

By filling your heart with constant praise you will quickly notice that worldly conversation has lost its appeal. By filling your heart with constant praise you will also notice a newfound joy and confidence in speaking with others about the kingdom of God. And by filling your heart with constant praise you will notice the power of God taking control of your life.

According to Scripture, the truly "good life," the "beautiful life," is a life of constantly praising God:

> "Praise the Lord! For it is good to sing praises to our God; for it is pleasant, and praise is beautiful" (Ps 147:1).

"It is good to give thanks to the Lord, and to sing praises to Your name, O Most High" (Ps 92:1).

"Rejoice in the Lord, O you righteous! For praise from the upright is beautiful" (Ps 33:1).

Wherever you are, whatever the situation, you can live the good life by praising God continuously with joyful song.

Every human is obligated to live for God's praise (Ps 150:6), and those who rejoice in this obligation identify themselves as "the people of God":

"But you are a chosen generation...His own special people, that [so that, in order that] you may proclaim the praises of Him who called you out of darkness into His marvelous light; who once were not a people but are now the people of God" (1Pet 2:9-10a).

When the Lord tells us, "Whoever offers praise glorifies Me," He shows us how to abide in what is most precious to Him. For those who truly love God, the highest experience of happiness is the joy of pleasing the Father through Christ, and we can do this continually by the sacrifice of praise to His name:

"Sing praises to His name, for it is pleasant" (Ps 135:3).

"I will praise the name of God with a song, and will magnify Him with thanksgiving. This also shall please the Lord" (Ps 69:30-31).

The true lovers of God testify openly:

"In God we boast all day long, and praise Your name forever" (Ps 44:8).

Are you facing great opposition from external circumstances or from struggles in your own heart? Start boasting in God all day long and watch what happens. Strongholds of opposition, both outside of you and within you, will come down by the power of God working through faith expressed in praise.

When we speak of praise we are speaking of faith. Praise is simply a bold expression of faith, and help is promised in time of need only to those who come boldly:

"Let us therefore come boldly to the throne of grace, that we may obtain mercy and find grace to help in time of need" (Heb 4:16).

"Christ Jesus our Lord, in whom we have boldness and access with confidence through faith in Him" (Eph 3:11b-12).

There is a faith that merely believes, but the faith that moves mountains is the faith that shouts aloud with joyful praise and refuses to stop.

Cling To Him In Praise!

From Genesis through Revelation the Scripture charges us to express our love and faith toward God with joyful praise. The more aggressively we rejoice, the more richly we enter God's power working through faith. Since Christ is our King, and since there is no law against rejoicing, we should awake in the morning to "break forth in song" and "praise Him according to His excellent greatness!" (Ps 98:4; 150:2).

The Scripture in Isaiah speaks of "those who rejoice in My exaltation" (13:3), and if we've nothing else to do we can joyfully thank the Lord for being alive to sing His praise.

The Scripture records that when Solomon became king "they blew the horn, and all the people said, "Long live King Solomon!" And all the people went up after him; and the people played the flutes and rejoiced with great joy, so that the earth seemed to split with their sound" (1Kings 1:39-40). If they rejoiced like this at the rise of Solomon, how much more should we rejoice at the exaltation of Jesus who said "a greater than Solomon is here"?! (Mt 12:42)

Again, if the people rejoiced with such aggression that "the earth seemed to split" when they "went up after Solomon," how much more should we split the earth and the skies and the seas as we joyfully run after Jesus?

The Lord has promised deliverance to those who cling to Him in love:

"Because he has set his love upon Me, therefore I will deliver him" (Ps 91:14-15)

There is no better way to focus our love on Christ than

47

to joyfully praise His name. "Let those also who love Your name be joyful in You" (Ps 5:11b). By clinging to Christ in praise we show that our love is set upon Him, and in this we see once again the connection between walking in praise and living in triumph.

We have seen how the Bible provides powerful examples of the Lord's people triumphing through praise against impossible odds. If your life is assaulted by problems beyond your strength and understanding, remember the examples of Jehoshaphat and Gideon and David and Paul and Silas. Without leaving other things undone, dare to put joyful praise ahead of every care, every effort, and every thought.

The Scripture in James warns that "a double-minded man" is "unstable in all his ways," and, "let not that man suppose that he will receive anything from the Lord" (1:7-8). The fullness of the blessing goes to those who live with single-minded commitment to God's glory in Christ, and for Christians who struggle with double-mindedness there is nothing like praise to focus the mind on Jesus alone.

By receiving the baptism into our Lord Jesus Christ we have taken a vow to war as soldiers against all that opposes the Father's glory in the Son. As Paul says to us all through Timothy:

> "You therefore must endure hardship as a good soldier of Jesus Christ. No one engaged in warfare entangles himself with the affairs of this life, that he may please him who enlisted him as a soldier" (2Tim 2:3-4).

By continuously praising God we leave no room in our hearts for entanglement with "the affairs of this life."

Our Lord warned of those "who hear the word, and the cares of this world, the deceitfulness of riches, and the desires for other things entering in choke the word, and it becomes unfruitful" (Mk 4:18-19). For all who struggle with the entanglements of double-mindedness, the remedy is praise. By constantly praising God a person becomes unable to mentally tolerate compromise, and constant praise will focus the mind for "bringing every thought into captivity to the obedience of Christ" (2Cor 10:5).

By diligent praise we uphold "the shield of faith with which you will be able to quench all the fiery darts of the wicked one" (Eph 6:16), and the Scripture also tells us in Proverbs:

"Keep your heart with all diligence, for out of it spring the issues of life" (4:23).

By constant praise we maintain a steadfast heart, as David testified when he "fled from Saul into the cave":

"My heart is steadfast, O God, my heart is steadfast; I will sing and give praise" (Ps 57:7).

Hiding in the cave like a cornered animal, David offered praise to keep his heart steady on God, and this provides yet another example of the power at work in our lives when we cling to God in praise.

Do you desire a more complete and richly satisfying experience of salvation? Once again the gateway to fullness is praise:

"But you shall call your walls Salvation, and
your gates Praise" (Isa 60:18b).

By entering the gates of praise we come to the walls of salvation. Knowing this, we should gladly say with the psalmist, "I will hope continually, and will praise You yet more and more" (71:14). At all times and in all situations the Scripture tells us to "make the voice of His praise to be heard" (Ps 66:8), and this is the wisdom of those who triumph through the name of the Lord.

The Scripture speaks of "the exceeding greatness of His power toward us who believe" (Eph 1:19). We are not told that God's power is great toward those who doubt. The fullness of life in Christ Jesus, with the "exceedingly great and precious promises" (2Pet 1:4), goes to those who "have faith and do not doubt." By filling our hearts with praise we grow strong in the faith that crushes doubt for a life of triumph in Christ Jesus our Lord.

Is your life afflicted with scarcity? Are you helpless and in need? The Scripture tells us in Psalms: "Let the poor and needy praise Your name" (74:21). In your time of scarcity give glory to God with the boldness of praise, and "the Father of mercies...shall supply all your need according to His riches in glory by Christ Jesus" (2Cor 1:3; Phil 4:19).

Without leaving other things undone, boldly put praise

Cling To Him In Praise!

ahead of every effort and every thought. Are you unemployed and badly in need of a job? Hit the pavement with steps of praise and God will direct your path to the greenest pasture. Do you lack confidence when being interviewed for a job? Fill your heart with joyful song all through the interview and God will seize control. As David sang "when he was in the wilderness of Judah" and greatly in need of help:

> "Because You have been my help, therefore in the shadow of Your wings I will rejoice" (Ps 63:7).

Wherever you are, however great the need and however helpless and overwhelmed you feel, fill your heart with melody to the Lord, rejoicing "in the shadow of His wings," knowing that God has promised "help in time of need" to those who come boldly. And, "Has He said, and will He not do? Or has He spoken, and will He not make it good?" (Num 23:19).

5

Give Thanks Always!!

"In everything give thanks; for this is the will of God in Christ Jesus for you." (1Thess 5:18)

Do your prayers seem weak and of little avail? If so, be encouraged to know the offering of thanks is Scripturally guaranteed to ignite your faith and fill your heart with the joy of pleasing God. The following study shows from Scripture how the continual giving of thanks will revolutionize your life and bring you deep into the fullness of God's promises in Christ.

The Lord "is rich to all who call upon Him" (Rom 10:12), and the proper way to call on Him is with the voice of thanksgiving:

> "I will offer to You the sacrifice of thanksgiving, and will call upon the name of the Lord" (Ps 116:17).

The Scripture records how in a time of great danger the prophet Daniel "prayed and gave thanks before his God, as was his custom since early days" (Dan 6:10), and on that same day Daniel was thrown into a den of lions where "no injury whatever was found on him, because he believed in his God" (vs 23). As a believer who relied on the Lord's favor in all situations, Daniel's custom was to lace his prayers with thanksgiving, showing us by example how we can bring to our hearts the fire of conviction when we pray.

When Jonah rebelled and was brought down under severe punishment, he prayed from "the fish's belly" and said, "I will sacrifice to You with the voice of thanksgiving" (Jonah 2:9). As with Daniel, the prophet Jonah offered his prayer with thanksgiving, and the following verse records the Lord's response:

> "So the Lord spoke to the fish, and it vomited
> Jonah onto dry land" (vs 10).

Whether we feel like Daniel, who had done nothing wrong but found himself in a den of lions, or like Jonah, who had done something wrong and found himself in the belly of a fish, we should learn from the prophets and call on the Lord "with the voice of thanksgiving." These Biblical examples show how expressions of gratitude accompany the faith by which all things are possible.

The Scriptures repeatedly emphasize the value of joyful thanksgiving in our approach to God:

"Let us come before His presence with thanks-giving; let us shout joyfully to Him with psalms" (Ps 95:2).

"Enter into His gates with thanksgiving, and into His courts with praise. Be thankful to Him, and bless His name" (Ps 100:4).

As the people of God we express our identity by a con-tinual offering of good works and praise (Tit 2:14; Eph 2:10; 1Pet 2:9). The giving of thanks relates closely to praise, and the two are often referred to interchangeably:

"I will give You thanks in the great assembly; I will praise You among many people" (Ps 35:18).

"Sing to the Lord with thanksgiving; sing praises on the harp to our God" (Ps 147:7).

The praise of thanksgiving expresses our righteousness in Christ:

"Surely the righteous shall give thanks to Your name" (Ps 140:13).

As the people of God, redeemed in righteousness by the blood of the Son, every mention or remembrance of the Lord's name should cause the voice of thanksgiving to rise in our hearts:

> "Sing praise to the Lord, you saints of His, and
> give thanks at the remembrance of His holy
> name" (Ps 30:4).

By giving thanks to His name we walk in the triumph
of praise:

> "(T)o give thanks to Your holy name, to tri-
> umph in Your praise" (Ps 106:47).

Joyful thanksgiving pours fuel on our spiritual flame to
burn away doubt that hinders "the power of God through faith."
When Jonah had no strength or wisdom for overcoming his impossible situation, he prayed with the voice of thanksgiving and
triumphed through the power of God. This was "written for our
learning" (Rom 15:4), and by the authority of Biblical example
we learn that deliverance and triumph are certain for those who
commit their lives to praising God with the voice of thanksgiving.

The Apostle Paul explained that everything we say and
do is to be an offering through Christ, but he emphasized that
whatever we offer must be accompanied by thanksgiving:

> "And whatever you do in word or deed, do all
> in the name of the Lord Jesus, giving thanks to
> God the Father through Him" (Col 3:17).

Only by giving thanks is our offering of word and deed

enriched by the name of Jesus.

The Epistle of James assures us "the effective, fervent prayer of a righteous man avails much" (5:16), but by comparing Scripture with Scripture we learn that "fervent prayer" is effective only when offered with thanks. As Paul tells us again in Colossians: "Continue earnestly in prayer, being vigilant in it with thanksgiving" (4:2). He writes of this again in Philippians, emphasizing how the full involvement of God for deliverance and triumph becomes our experience only when prayer is offered with thanksgiving:

> "Be anxious for nothing, but in everything by prayer and supplication, with thanksgiving, let your requests be made known to God; and the peace of God, which surpasses all understanding, will guard your hearts and minds through Christ Jesus." (4:6-7).

When we are helpless and without strength to change a situation, the prayer of aggressive thanksgiving drives out anxiety and brings to our hearts an outpouring of joyful peace that surpasses understanding. This is not the peace of an ostrich sticking its head in the sand to ignore the threatening issues; rather, it is the peace of knowing that God has seized control of our situation and is accomplishing the good that we ourselves could not hope to accomplish.

The Apostle Paul gave enormous emphasis to thanksgiving in relation to prayer and to the whole of Christian living. The following is a brief sampling from his Epistles, and we urge attention to the link between effective prayer and the giving of thanks:

To the Christians in Rome: "First, I thank my God through Jesus Christ for you all" (1:8).

To those in Corinth: "I thank my God always concerning you" (1Cor 1:4).

To those in Ephesus: "I...do not cease to give thanks for you, making mention of you in my prayers" (1:15-16).

To those in Philippi: "I thank my God upon every remembrance of you, always in every prayer of mine making request for you all with joy" (1:3-4).

To those in Colosse: "We give thanks to the God and Father of our Lord Jesus Christ, praying always for you" (1:3).

To those in Thessalonica: "We give thanks to God always for you all, making mention of you in our prayers" (1Th 1:2). "For this reason we also thank God without ceasing" (1Th 2:13). "We are bound to thank God always for you, brethren" (2Th 1:3).

To Timothy: "I exhort first of all that supplications, prayers, intercessions, and giving of thanks be made for all men" (1Tim 2:1). "I thank my God...as without ceasing I remember you in my prayers night and day" (2Tim 1:3).

To Philemon: "I thank my God, making mention of you always in my prayers" (vs 4).

The Bible consistently links thanksgiving with the power of God working through prayer. Joyful thanksgiving is a show of boldness, expressing to God our confidence in His promise to act. If heartfelt expressions of gratitude have been lacking in your prayers, you will experience your own spiritual revival by committing your heart and tongue to a consistent outpouring of thanks.

A failure to be thankful, even in extreme adversity, places a person outside the will of God:

"In everything give thanks; for this is the will of God in Christ Jesus for you" (1Th 5:18).

In telling us to give thanks in all things, Paul shows that continual thanksgiving brings everything that concerns us into the hand of God, and only by giving thanks do we keep ourselves in His will for the guarantee of His favor. But the person who withholds thanksgiving shows unbelief, and "let not that man suppose that he will receive anything from the Lord" (Js 1:7).

The giving of thanks is described in Scripture as a spiritual sacrifice to be offered with joy:

"Let them sacrifice the sacrifices of thanksgiving, and declare His works with rejoicing" (Ps 107:22).

By constantly praising God with joyful thanksgiving we also fill our hearts with light to walk in the confidence of His leading:

> "Blessed are the people who know the joyful sound! They walk, O Lord, in the light of Your countenance. In Your name they rejoice all day long" (Ps 89:15-16).

Does your life seem so complicated that you "don't know what to do?" The wisdom of Scripture instructs you to rejoice all day for the light of the Lord's countenance to shine on your path.

> "In all your ways acknowledge Him, and He shall direct your paths" (Prov 3:6).

There is no better way to acknowledge Him than to joyfully thank Him for the promise. In the offering of praise we have made the acknowledgment, but when praise is withheld there is no acknowledgment and we forfeit the guarantee.

When you are faced with a decision, whether big or small, rejoice with thanksgiving for the Lord's promise to fill your heart with wisdom and to "lead you in the paths of righteousness for His name's sake."

The Scripture condemns the world for refusing to offer the praise of thanksgiving, saying in Romans that "they are without excuse, because, although they knew God, they did not glorify Him as God, nor were thankful, but became futile in their thoughts, and their foolish hearts were darkened" (1:20-21). Ingratitude is a fruit of unbelief and leads to further mental decay. In contrast, by continually thanking God we fill our hearts with light that leads to sound thinking in all things.

Under the old covenant, with its great emphasis on animal sacrifice, the offering of thanks was more pleasing to God than the sacrifice of bulls and goats:

> "I will praise the name of God with a song, and will magnify Him with thanksgiving. This also shall please the Lord better than an ox or bull" (Ps 69:30-31).

As the sheep of Christ we are able to please and magnify God at all times with the voice of thanksgiving:

> "So we, Your people and sheep of Your pasture, will give You thanks forever" (Ps 79:13).

Every moment of wakefulness provides opportunity to magnify God with the praise of thanksgiving:

> "At midnight I will rise to give thanks to You" (Ps 119:62).

As believers in the goodness of God, thanksgiving should be the atmosphere of our thoughts and conversation, "singing and making melody in your heart to the Lord, giving thanks always for all things to God the Father in the name of our Lord Jesus Christ" (Eph 5:19-20). Thanksgiving should saturate our speech and characterize our lifestyle, as Paul says again when he exhorts us to not indulge in "foolish talking, nor course jesting, which are not fitting, but rather giving of thanks" (Eph 5:4).

By offering thanks we express our confidence that God is good:

> "Oh, give thanks to the Lord, for He is good!" (Ps 106:1a).

For those who love Christ, the great value of living is the opportunity to glorify God and to please Him continually with songs of gratitude. This is the truly good life:

> "It is good to give thanks to the Lord, and to sing praises to Your name" (Ps 92:1).

The Psalmist asks to be delivered from death in order to continue giving thanks:

> "For in death there is no remembrance of You; in the grave who will give You thanks?" (Ps 6:5).

Wherever we are, in whatever situation, we can live the good life by praising God with songs of thanksgiving. As Paul, who gave thanks "without ceasing," testified in a letter written from jail: "I have learned in whatever state I am, to be content" (Phil 4:11). As Christians we are able to invest every moment with eternal value by filling the moment with the praise of thanksgiving.

By the continual giving of thanks our faith takes wings and all things become possible. When Jesus gave thanks for the seven loaves, the power of God multiplied the food for feeding a multitude:

> "And He took the seven loaves and the fish and gave thanks, broke them and gave them to His disciples; and the disciples gave to the multitude. So they all ate and were filled" (Mt 15:36-37a).

The Scripture in John refers to this as "the place where they ate bread after the Lord had given thanks" (6:23), emphasizing the relevance of thanksgiving in the conversion of scarcity into abundance.

This spiritual knowledge shows that the most sensible thing any of us can do is to constantly offer this sacrifice to God:

> "Therefore by (Christ) let us continually offer the sacrifice of praise to God, that is, the fruit of our lips, giving thanks to His name" (Heb 13:15).

As Christians, we must emphasize joyful thanksgiving without making light of one another's difficulties:

"Rejoice with those who rejoice, and weep
with those who weep" (Rom 12:15).

As Paul also testified in Second Corinthians:

"Blessed be the…Father of mercies and God of
all comfort, who comforts us in all our tribulation, that we may be able to comfort those who
are in any trouble" (1:3-4).

To encourage a person in pain we must enter spiritually
into his hurt:

"Bear one another's burdens, and so fulfill the
law of Christ" (Gal 6:2).

But even in the roughest of times we must exhort one
another with powerful encouragements to offer praise and
thanksgiving, knowing our Shepherd and King is deeply involved and has promised to act when we call:

"Call upon Me in the day of trouble; I will deliver you, and you shall glorify Me" (Ps 50:15).

By calling on Him with the voice of thanksgiving we
number ourselves with the priests and the prophets and with all
who "call upon Him in truth":

"Oh, give thanks to the Lord! Call upon His

name…Samuel was among those who called
upon His name; they called upon the Lord, and
He answered them" (Ps 105:1; 99:6).

We have repeatedly seen in Scripture how praise and
thanksgiving bind us to the Lord's name for the guarantee of
His favor in our time of need. By the offering of thanks we call
on the Lord in truth and we can confidently say with David:

"The Lord will hear when I call to Him" (Ps 4:3).

And:

"In the day of my trouble I will call upon You,
for You will answer me…For You, Lord, are
good…and abundant in mercy to all those who
call upon You" (Ps 86:7,5).

We show the brokenness of absolute trust by offering
thanks to the Father in times of pain and sorrow, knowing that
He "is near to those who have a broken heart, and saves such as
have a contrite spirit" (Ps 34:18). By giving thanks to Him always we show the humility of those whom He delights to deliver:

"I dwell in the high and holy place, with him
who has a contrite and humble spirit, to revive
the spirit of the humble, and to revive the heart
of the contrite ones" (Isa 57:15).

The world of the unbelieving relies on its own wisdom and refuses the brokenness of grateful praise, but believers in Christ show the wisdom of salvation by falling before Him in joyful worship for the goodness of His word. As He says again in Isaiah:

> "But on this one will I look: on him who is poor and of a contrite spirit, and who trembles at My word" (66:2).

In our seasons of pain we do not enjoy the hurt itself, but we rejoice in His assurance that "all things work together for good to those who love God." The Scripture tells us we should be "giving thanks always for all things," and "in everything give thanks." If we truly believe that "all things" work together for our good, we will gladly give thanks in "all things."

Under the old covenant law of sacrifice, the offerings brought to God had to be without blemish:

> "And whoever offers a sacrifice…it must be perfect to be accepted; there shall be no defect in it" (Lev 22:21).

> "But if there is a defect in it, if it is lame or blind or has any serious defect, you shall not sacrifice it to the Lord your God" (Dt 15:21).

A prayer offered without thanksgiving is defective. It is

a sacrifice with blemish.

      If your prayers have seemed dry and ineffectual, dash them with the salt of thanksgiving for a flavor well-pleasing to God. By giving thanks to Him always you will triumph in His praise, and like Daniel the prophet you will walk among lions with no fear of harm.

6

Dare To Rejoice!

*"I smile at my enemies, because I rejoice
in Your salvation." (1Sam 2:1)*

Do you wonder how seriously the Father regards your prayers? Although you know you are saved, does it seem that your voice is small in the kingdom of God? In this chapter you will learn from the Scriptures how the voice of rejoicing is delightful to the Lord, and you will learn how greatly you can honor Him at all times and in all situations. No matter how small or oppressed you have felt in the past, you can become an instant giant walking in triumph by the boldness of faith expressed in joyful praise.

The reign of God is a rock of confidence for all who believe. After Joseph's brothers had sold him into slavery he suffered years of anguish:

"Joseph...was sold as a slave. They hurt his feet with fetters, he was laid in irons. Until the time that His word came to pass, the word of the Lord tested him" (Ps 105:17-19).

When Joseph gained the upper hand and his brothers approached him with trembling, he told them, "Do not be afraid...you meant evil against me; but God meant it for good" (Gen 50:19-20). This example illustrates the bedrock of our confidence for rejoicing in even the worst of times: GOD OUR KING IS GOOD. Because He reigns, and because He is good, those who put their trust in Him will boldly rejoice in His name. As the Scriptures abundantly testify:

"The Lord reigns; let the earth rejoice; let the multitude of isles be glad" (Ps 97:1).

"Oh, clap your hands, all you peoples! Shout to God with the voice of triumph! For the Lord Most High is awesome; He is a great King over all the earth" (Ps 47:1-2).

Whoever approaches the Lord is expected to rejoice:

"Sing to God, sing praises to His name...and rejoice before Him" (Ps 68:4).

In ancient kingdoms a person risked execution for approaching the king with a sad expression, as this threatened the king's idea of himself as the provider of security, riches and happiness for the subjects of his realm. The Biblical writer Nehemiah recorded his fear after showing sadness at the table of King Artaxerxes (Nehemiah served as the king's cupbearer):

> "Now I had never been sad in his presence before. Therefore the king said to me, "Why is your face sad, since you are not sick? This is nothing but sorrow of heart." So I became dreadfully afraid" (Neh 2:1b-2).

His being "dreadfully afraid" shows the seriousness of his breach of culture, and although this custom in the presence of ancient kings was pretentious and vain, it helps to illustrate the proper way to approach the King of kings:

> "Serve the Lord with gladness; come before His presence with singing" (Ps 100:2).

> "Let us come before His presence with thanksgiving; let us shout joyfully to Him with psalms" (Ps 95:2).

Our joyful praise in the presence of God expresses delight in His goodness and confidence in His rule. But a failure to rejoice shows unbelief, and "without faith it is impossible to please Him" (Heb 11:6).

The Scripture tells us that, "Honor and majesty are before Him: strength and gladness are in His place" (1Chron

16:27). By coming to Him without gladness we have no share in His strength, and by refusing to rejoice in His presence we cast insults at His majesty. If we truly aim to honor the Lord and to enjoy the fullness of His favor, we will rejoice before Him with passion and confidence in all situations.

The Scripture in Romans tells us to "render therefore to all their due; taxes to whom taxes...honor to whom honor" (13:7). Because God is the true and righteous King, all the earth is commanded to honor Him with joyful praises:

> "Make a joyful shout to God, all the earth! Sing out the honor of His name; make His praise glorious" (Ps 66:1-2).

> "Make a joyful shout to the Lord, all you lands!" (Ps 100:1).

If you have felt small and irrelevant to the work of the kingdom, you can change this right now with the decision to "break forth in song, rejoice, and...shout joyfully before the Lord, the King" (Ps 98:4,6).

The prophet Isaiah acknowledged to God that, "You meet him who rejoices and does righteousness" (Isa 64:5). Do you want God's attention? You can have it immediately by lifting your voice and flooding His throne with "sacrifices of joy." This is how David brought his prayer to God's throne when "the wicked came against me to eat up my flesh":

> "I will offer sacrifices of joy in His tabernacle;

I will sing, yes, I will sing praises to the Lord.
Hear, O Lord, when I cry with my voice!" (Ps
27:2,6-7a).

David understood that the Lord "is a rewarder of those
who diligently seek Him" (Heb 11:6), but that He meets only
with those who seek Him joyfully.

If it seems that your prayers have been met with silence, cry out to God with the voice of rejoicing and He will
meet you with abundance.

Joyful praise is God's rightful due as the good Shepherd and the faithful King, and those who bring this delightful
worship are the sons who live boldly by faith for the praise of
His glory:

"This people I have formed for Myself; they
shall declare My praise" (Isa 43:21).

By joyfully praising God we identify ourselves as the
people who live in His presence, but a voice that refuses to rejoice in His name is not worthy of being heard at His throne.

David cried out in the wasteland of the wilderness, "My
mouth shall praise You with joyful lips" (Ps 63:5), and those
who have faith will learn to live before God with joy at all
times:

"In Your name they rejoice all day long" (Ps 89:16).

Not only in the day, but all through the night:

"Let the saints be joyful in glory; let them sing aloud on their beds" (Ps 149:5).

Everything we say or do is to be offered to God through Christ (Col 3:17), but the offering must be accompanied with thanksgiving and joyful passion: "And whatever you do, do it heartily, as to the Lord and not to men" (Col 3:23).

This was the commandment given to Israel after the deliverance from Egypt:

"You shall rejoice before the Lord your God in all to which you put your hands" (Dt 12:18).

But Israel did not do this, and Moses prophetically warned:

"Because you did not serve the Lord your God with joy and gladness of heart...therefore you shall serve your enemies" (Dt 28:47-48a).

By refusing to live with joy we hand to our enemies a foothold, but we can smile at adversity by rejoicing in the Lord. No matter what the situation or how greatly the odds stack against you, the wisdom of Scripture instructs you to "shout to God with the voice of triumph!" (Ps 47:1). Without leaving other things undone, step boldly into the day and believe the word that promises "triumph in Your praise" (1Chron 16:35).

The enemy of faith is doubt, and it is doubt that hinders "the power of God through faith" and keeps us away from "the

favor You have toward Your people" (Ps 106:4). Are you serv-
ing your enemies? If so, joyful praise is the way out. Whatever
adversities and threats are coming against you, there is no opposition equal to God's power working through faith expressed
in joyful praise.

The Lord "rules by His power forever" (Ps 66:7a), and
by rejoicing in Him we boldly express our delight in His goodness and our confidence in His power. There is no law to prevent you from rejoicing in Christ at all times "with joy inexpressible and full of glory" (1Pet 1:8).

When the shepherds of Bethlehem returned to their
fields they were "glorifying and praising God" after seeing the
Child whom the angel had announced with "good tidings of
great joy" (Lk 2:20,10). Have we allowed these tidings to grow
stale in our hearts? Is there any legitimate reason for our joy in
these tidings to diminish? If the birth of our Shepherd and King
has become "old news" to us, we can experience the freshness
of the tidings by rejoicing and giving thanks to the Father for
the birth of the Son, singing songs of celebration to the glory of
God from sun-up till sundown and all through the night.

When the wise men came "from the East" to see Jesus
soon after His birth, a miraculous star "came and stood over
where the young Child was," and when the wise men "saw the
star, they rejoiced with exceedingly great joy" (Mt 2:1,9-10). If
the wise men rejoiced with such joy after verifying the birth of
the King, why should we not rejoice with even greater joy since
Christ is not only born but has died for our sins and risen to
reign forever?

Rejoicing is a weapon of war that strengthens our faith

for pulling down strongholds, and our faith grows exceedingly bold as we offer the sacrifice of joy continuously. Regardless of our circumstance or the adversity in our lives, we should say with the prophet Habakkuk, "I will rejoice in the Lord, I will joy in the God of my salvation." We should do this all day, any day, every day. We should do this because "the Lord Most High is awesome; He is a great King over all the earth" (Ps 47:2).

But if we are not rejoicing in the word of the Lord, we show that we do not really believe it. A failure to rejoice is simply a failure of faith.

Joyful worship expresses our true identity in the righteousness of faith:

> "The righteous shall be glad in the Lord and trust in Him" (Ps 64:10).

> "Be glad in the Lord and rejoice, you righteous; and shout for joy, all you upright in heart" (Ps 32:11).

We boldly show who we are by rejoicing aggressively in the name of Jesus at all times in all situations:

> "Rejoice in the Lord always. Again I will say, rejoice!" (Phil 4:4)

> "But let the righteous be glad; let them rejoice before God; yes, let them rejoice exceed-

ingly" (Ps 68:3).

By continual rejoicing we embolden our faith for seizing the favor shown to the righteous, and as often as we remember His name we should rejoice and give thanks:

> "Rejoice in the Lord, you righteous, and give thanks at the remembrance of His holy name" (Ps 97:12).

If your life is afflicted with adverse circumstances, you have all the more opportunity to glorify God with joyful praise and to thank Him continuously as He takes control of your situation.

For a believer, circumstances do not determine the true quality of life on this passing earth. The world of the unbelieving will not agree because "the natural man does not receive the things of the Spirit of God, for they are foolishness to him" (1Cor 2:14). The apostle who wrote these words to the Corinthians also said in another letter:

> "I have learned in whatever state I am, to be content: I know how to be abased, and I know how to abound. Everywhere and in all things I have learned both to be full and to be hungry, both to abound and to suffer need" (Phil 4:11-12).

When Paul wrote this letter to the Philippian Christians

his body was burdened with chains and hemmed in by prison walls, and his problems were further compounded by agitators "supposing to add affliction to my chains" (1:16). In this lowly and painful circumstance he beautified his life with joyful praise, showing by example how the truly good life is the one whose days are filled with rejoicing in Christ no matter what the external conditions.

Paul exhorts us to not, under any circumstance, complain. He tells us in Philippians to "do all things without complaining and disputing, that you may become blameless and harmless, children of God without fault in the midst of a crooked and perverse generation, among whom you shine as lights in the world" (Phil 2:14-15). By choosing to rejoice rather than complain we mark ourselves as God's children who "shine as lights in the world." But when we complain we are in defeat, giving ground to the enemy, failing as sons of the King.

A complaining person cannot say, "(T)hrough Your name we will trample those who rise up against us" (Ps 44:5). A complaining person has forsaken the boldness of joy and is resisting "the power of God through faith." Complaining is a show of unhealthy faith, or of no faith at all, since a person cannot complain and walk in faith at the same time.

The voice of complaining belongs to the world of unbelief, but the power of God works through a voice that thunders with faith.

The Scripture exhorts us to "take up the whole armor of God...and having done all, to stand" (Eph 6:13). We do not stand by complaining. We stand by joyful faith that exalts the word of God above all the logic of the world.

Dare To Rejoice!

If your life is assaulted by problems beyond your strength and understanding, dare to put the praise of rejoicing ahead of everything. No matter how absurd your joyful faith might appear to the world around you, cling to God with steadfast rejoicing and He will vindicate your confession.

By endurance in rejoicing we run strong to the finish:

"But none of these (tribulations) move me; nor
do I count my life dear to myself, so that I may
finish my race with joy" (Acts 20:24).

By racing with joy we make our whole life a sprint to the crown of glory that waits at the finish.

The Scripture in Romans describes the kingdom of God as a realm of "joy in the Holy Spirit" (14:17), teaching us that rejoicing in Christ is the culture of the kingdom, and that faith without joy gives only a partial experience of the fullness that Christ has brought.

For those who have Biblical faith, the true value of life is centered in praise and not in external conditions. By a lifestyle of joyful praise our conditions become our servant as the power of God works through faith to bring abundance from scarcity, never doubting that the desert will blossom as we fill our days with rejoicing from beginning to end. Although we are thankful for pleasant circumstances, and we should aggressively pursue opportunities to enrich the lives of others in the name of Jesus, the true source of our joy is not in passing pleasures but in "the word of our God" which "abides forever."

"(H)e who is of a merry heart has a continual

feast" (Prov 15:15), and there is no circumstance that can threaten the feast of those who rejoice in the Lord "as one who finds great treasure" (Ps 119:162). As Paul also instructed by example: "Everywhere and in all things...rejoice in the Lord" (Phil 4:12; 3:1). When we live without joy we will struggle with unhealthy faith, but by filling our hearts with joyful faith we have an endless feast.

The Scripture tells us in Proverbs:

"Anxiety in the heart of man causes depression,
but a good word makes it glad" (12:25).

The good word is Jesus Christ from Genesis through Revelation, and for those who believe in Him there is no excuse for defeat because the Almighty God our Father has authorized us to rejoice.

If your life is dry, intimidating, or painful, there is no law to prevent you from leaping for joy at God's treasure in Christ (Gal 5:22-23). There is no law to prevent you from joyfully celebrating "as men rejoice when they divide the spoil," or as those who rejoice "according to the joy of harvest" (Isa 9:3). There is nothing at all to prevent you from launching immediately into a life of joyful triumph through constant praise in the name of Christ. By continually offering songs of joy your life will become a sustained celebration of the Father's glory in the Son.

In the world you will have adversity, but in a stressful situation there is no better policy than to joyfully sing to God.

If your spirit is dull and your life oppressed, you will

experience a dramatic change on every front by filling your days with the sacrifice of joyful praise. Regardless of how small and painful your life has felt, exalt the Lord with joyful song and the Father of mercies will meet you richly with the favor He shows to the righteous.

Twenty centuries ago a virgin gave birth to the Son of God, and several decades later He died for our sins and rose to the Father's right hand where He leads as our Shepherd and reigns as our King. Through the boldness of faith you can joyfully celebrate the day of His birth, and you can rejoice exceedingly in the day He was seen alive from the dead. You can rejoice with those whom He healed and be glad with those whom He raised, and you can joyfully walk with Him in the wind and the rain on the waves of the sea.

7

Rejoicing Through Sorrow

"The sacrifices of God are a broken spirit,
a broken and a contrite heart—these, O God,
You will not despise." (Ps 51:17)

Is your grief so severe that you can no longer relate to the experience of joy? Have the blows of loss and failure left you unsure that a better life is even possible? In this chapter you will learn from Biblical example how your suffering can become an offering to God who is deeply involved for your good. We will look at Scriptures that assure us the Lord "is near to those who have a broken heart" (Ps 34:18), and how the sacrifice of a broken spirit will never be turned away at the throne of Almighty God.

Jesus, "who for the joy that was set before Him endured the cross" (Heb 12:2), demonstrated the power of joy that comes through faith no matter how dark the hour. The prophet Isaiah described Him as "a Man of sorrows and acquainted with grief" (Isa 53:3), but Jesus spoke also of a joy the world cannot experience, a joy found only in Him by those who abide in His word:

> "These things I have spoken to you, that My joy may remain in you, and that your joy may be full" (Jn 15:11).

Jesus described this fullness of joy as something the world cannot take away, saying to the disciples on the night of His betrayal:

> "Therefore you now have sorrow; but I will see you again [after three days in the grave] and your heart will rejoice, and your joy no one will take from you" (Jn 16:22).

When Jesus spoke this way about the joy experienced by those who believe, the Lord Himself was "sorrowful and deeply distressed," saying to the disciples in the Garden of Gethsemane:

> "My soul is exceedingly sorrowful, even to death" (Mt 26:38).

But He had just finished a prayer in which He said:

"I come to You, and these things I speak in the
world, that they may have My joy fulfilled in
themselves" (Jn 17:13).

While "exceedingly sorrowful," Jesus prayed that all
who believe would experience the fullness of the joy that filled
His own heart. This is "the joy of the Lord" that comes only
through faith in the assurance that "all things work together for
good to those who love God" (Rom 8:28). Because Jesus per-
fected obedience He rejoiced with perfect assurance that His
suffering was an instrument through which enormous good
would be accomplished, and we who believe also have access
to this wellspring of joy through faith in His righteous name.

In the exhortation to worship with joyful praise at all
times, we do not make light of sorrow. "Jesus wept" (Jn 11:35),
and in this world of pain we too will weep. But we do not sorrow with "the sorrow of the world" (2Cor 7:10); instead, we
offer our tears with joyful cries of gratitude for God's promise
of good through all that we suffer. A Christian trained in the
Scriptures will show tender respect for pain and sorrow while
encouraging the sufferer to cast his burden on the Lord by joyfully giving thanks. As James tells us:

"My brethren, count it all joy when you fall
into various trials" (Js 1:2).

But sometimes the trials are 'beyond measure,' and in
times such as these we face the question of how far we can live
by faith? Is there a limit? Do you feel that your pain and loss

are just too much? Does it seem unreasonable to even think of rejoicing? In your great trial of pain you will need to decide whether the word of God is always true, or only sometimes true.

When Job was hit with the pain of enormous loss, he "fell to the ground and worshiped. And he said: "...The Lord gave, and the Lord has taken away; blessed be the name of the Lord"" (Job 1:20-21). Controversy has sometimes swirled around this passage in Job, but we know with Biblical certainty that when Job made this statement he "did not sin nor charge God with wrong" (vs 22). Although we cannot explain the full mystery, we know that our God is somehow involved for our good in the tragedies we suffer.

In a season of great sorrow (his children were killed), Job did not give pleasure to Satan by doubting the goodness of God. He did not "charge God with wrong," but he acknowledged that the goodness of God was stronger than his pain and would somehow prevail to the praise of God's glory if Job would stay faithful. Job, the suffering saint, declared his righteousness by offering praise in a time of tragic distress, and the Scripture later testifies how "the Lord blessed the latter days of Job more than his beginning" (42:12).

However great your pain, and however deep your loss, you can reach out to God with tears on your fingers and rejoice with confidence that His word of promise is stronger than your grief.

Praising God in a time of sorrow is not a "positive mental affirmation." It is a bold confession of faith in the goodness of God and in His faithfulness to shepherd our lives

through the hardest of times. The great lesson of Job's experience is summarized in the Book of James, showing us once
again that in times of trial we can reach with our pain for the
word of assurance that God is involved for our good:

> "Indeed we count them blessed who endure.
> You have heard of the perseverance of Job and
> seen the end intended by the Lord—that the
> Lord is very compassionate and merci-
> ful" (5:11).

As Christians, we do not endure adversity with 'gritted
teeth'. Rather, in times of sorrow we worship through tears and
"give thanks to Your holy name, to triumph in Your
praise" (1Chron 16:35). But only the mind of faith can reason
with the logic of joy in a time of great affliction.

Peter also wrote to Christians under trial, saying in his
First Epistle:

> "In this (salvation) you greatly rejoice, though
> now for a little while, if need be, you have been
> grieved by various trials" (1:6).

Although these Christians were "grieved by trials,"
they continued to "greatly rejoice," and Peter applauds their
faith when he writes in the same passage:

> "Jesus Christ, whom having not seen you love.
> Though now you do not see Him, yet believing,

you rejoice with joy inexpressible and full of glory" (vs 8).

In the grief of trial they rejoiced exceedingly in the Lord's promise to accomplish good through all that they suffered. While showing full respect for the pain of affliction, they encouraged one another with assurances of faith in the goodness and power of God.

Sorrow is legitimate for Christians in a passing world, but as we develop our spiritual understanding we learn to walk on stormy water with our eyes fixed on Jesus. The heart of a growing believer is a sponge absorbing the joyful presence of Christ and praising Him with confidence for the favor He shows to those who come boldly. We do not rejoice in the suffering itself. We rejoice in our Lord's assurance that every tear is in His book and no adversity can separate us from His loving promise to order all things for our good. By having the boldness to rejoice while in the greatest pain we march through our days in the power of triumph as "more than conquerors through Him who loved us" (Rom 8:37).

The Scripture guarantees triumph through an unbroken walk of praise which leads also to a life of good works in greater abundance. A life of fruitfulness is not what saves us; rather, this is the purpose for which we are saved (Tit 2:14; Eph 2:10; Jn 15:8). Whatever comes against you, no matter how hurt or how helpless you feel, cling to God in praise and live with confidence in all He has promised through Jesus Christ our Lord.

The Apostle Paul repeatedly demonstrated this strength of joy in difficult times, saying in Colossians: "I now rejoice in my sufferings for you" (1:24). And in Second Corinthians: "I am exceedingly joyful in all our tribulation" (7:4). As he said also to the Christians of Thessalonica:

> "And you became followers of us and of the Lord, having received the word in much affliction, with joy of the Holy Spirit" (1Th 1:6).

The Book of Hebrews was written to Christians who "endured a great struggle with sufferings...and joyfully accepted the plundering of your goods" (10:32,34). Their unpleasant experience of being plundered provided opportunity for glorifying God by rejoicing in a time of distress. These Christians would not have enjoyed the suffering itself, but with boldness of faith they rejoiced with confidence that "the Lord is my Shepherd" and "I shall not want." These afflicted believers were exhorted to "hold fast the confidence and the rejoicing of the hope firm to the end" (3:6), being assured that God "is a rewarder of those who diligently seek Him" (11:6).

Sorrow and affliction are no threat to the joyful faith of those who live boldly for Christ, as Paul testified yet again when he spoke of being "sorrowful, yet always rejoicing" (2Cor 6:10). When the Lord said to Paul in a time of infirmity, "My strength is made perfect in weakness" (2Cor 12:9), Paul rejoiced in this word so boldly that even his weakness became an avenue for the power of Christ:

> "Therefore most gladly I will rather boast in my infirmities, that the power of Christ may

Kings of Praise

rest upon me. Therefore I take pleasure in infir-
mities, in reproaches, in needs, in persecutions,
in distresses, for Christ's sake. For when I am
weak, then I am strong" (2Cor 12:9-10).

Paul had previously viewed his infirmity as an obstacle
to the fullness of life, telling us how he had "pleaded with the
Lord three times that it might depart" (2Cor 12:8). By learning
to "take pleasure" in his infirmity the power of Christ multiplied in Paul's life and ministry, not because he enjoyed the
distress of the infirmity but rather because he rejoiced in the
assurance that "all things work together for good to those who
love God." By rejoicing through times of great affliction he
brought to maturity the faith by which all things are possible,
and even his affliction became an instrument of power for the
edification of many to the glory of God.

If you are spiritually discouraged because of infirmity,
or adversity, or failure in your life, be encouraged to know the
one-step remedy for chronic spiritual weakness is the leap into
a lifestyle of praising God. Fear and depression, discouragement and sorrow, cannot stand in the presence of praise. As the
psalmist says again:

"Why are you cast down, O my soul? And why
are you disquieted within me? [He has slipped
into worry and depression, but he knows the
remedy:] Hope in God; for I shall yet praise
Him, the help of my countenance and my
God" (Ps 42:11).

90

The power of God works through faith, and the walk of faith is purified by continual rejoicing. By feeding the heart with joy our faith takes wings to say with the persecuted psalmist: "By my God I can leap over a wall" (18:29). And with the imprisoned apostle: "I can do all things through Christ who strengthens me" (Phil 4:13). And with Mary before the physical evidence of the promise: "He who is mighty has done great things for me" (Lk 1:49).

All of these rejoiced in God's word "as one who finds great treasure," and none of these believed that adverse circumstances could threaten the Lord's ability to perform what He had promised. In the face of doubt they joyfully shouted, "Let God be true but every man a liar" (Rom 3:4). This is the faith that moves mountains and causes human feet to walk on water.

Our Lord assured us that "in the world you will have tribulation" (Jn 16:33). The triumphant life of exceeding joy is no cakewalk for the flesh, as Paul affirmed in describing the pilgrimage of those who learned through Scripture and through experience to "rejoice in the Lord always":

> "For we do not want you to be ignorant, brethren, of our trouble which came to us in Asia: that we were burdened beyond measure, above strength, so that we despaired even of life. Yes, we had the sentence of death in ourselves, that we should not trust in ourselves but in God who raises the dead" (2Cor 1:8-9).

And:

"We are hard-pressed on every side, yet not crushed; we are perplexed, but not in despair; persecuted, but not forsaken; struck down, but not destroyed" (2Cor 4:8-9).

Are you hard-pressed and baffled? Do you feel struck down and torn on the inside? You can make your pain an offering to God by sacrifices of praise for His promise of good through all that you suffer. Even in the harshest of times you can worship through tears and overcome the world by joyful shouts of confidence in the name of Jesus.

When the power of grief has crushed your vision of what could still be possible, and when pain and helplessness leave you small and with no sense of adequacy for the demands of life, you can lift up your soul to kiss the words of Him who spoke of joy while He was "exceedingly sorrowful, even to death." You can do this because the Lord is your Shepherd and He is with you. You can do this in the darkest hour of the coldest night. You can do this right now.

8

Rejoicing With Song!

"Therefore I will play music
before the Lord" (2Sam 6:21).

Are you struggling with spiritual motivation? Do you have addictions that cripple your spiritual life? Or do you simply feel inadequate for the work of ministry among the needy people of your community? In this chapter you will learn how the offering of song results in spiritual growth and mighty outpourings of "the power of God through faith." No matter where you are or what your situation, the Holy Spirit will take control of your life as you offer "psalms and hymns and spiritual songs, singing with grace in your hearts to the Lord" (Col 3:16).

When Paul and Silas had received "many stripes" and been thrown "into the inner prison" with "their feet in the stocks," they sang to God "with a voice of triumph" that shook the earth and shattered the chains (cf. Acts 16:22-26; 2Cor 2:14; Ps 47:1). All of this was "written for our learning" (Rom 15:4) to show us how all things are possible for those who live by "the power of God through faith" expressed in songs of praise.

To make a noise to God in the name of Christ is an aggressive show of confidence and affection, and believers are often urged in Scripture to "make a joyful shout to God" (Ps 66:1). The following verses bring emphasis to the boldness of faith expressed in making a joyful noise to celebrate the Father's glory in the Son:

> "Shout joyfully to the Lord, all the earth; break forth in song, rejoice, and sing praises" (Ps 98:4).

> "Sing to God, sing praises to His name" (Ps 68:4).

> "Make a joyful shout to the Lord, all you lands!" (Ps 100:1).

> "Oh, let the nations be glad and sing for joy!" (Ps 67:4).

> "(L)et Your saints shout for joy" (Ps 132:9).

> "Blessed are the people who know the joyful sound!" (Ps 89:15).

"Praise Him with loud cymbals; praise Him with clashing cymbals! Let everything that has breath praise the Lord" (Ps 150:5-6).

By songs of praise we offer to God the fullness of worship, as when the priests under the old covenant were appointed "to offer the burnt offerings of the Lord...with rejoicing and with singing" (2Chron 23:18). With shouts and songs, as well as by quiet melody in the heart, you will perfect your offering to the Father through Jesus, and the song within you should be for Him and for Him alone. As the psalmist confessed:

"Therefore my heart greatly rejoices, and with my song I will praise Him" (Ps 28:7).

God has ordained music as a powerful expression of faith and love, and if you seriously desire to "grow in the grace and knowledge" of Christ you will fill your heart continually with "psalms and hymns and spiritual songs."

Believers should be cautious about music that does not aim to celebrate the goodness of God and "His wonderful works to the children of men" (Ps 107:21). It is the nature of the case that worldly music identifies with the god of this world, and a Christian places his or herself at enormous spiritual risk by receiving into the mind what is knowingly "not of the Father but is of the world" (cf. 1Jn 2:15-17). Each of us must decide what we will do, but there is no godly wisdom in throwing open the doors of the mind to the seductive influence of music that does not aim to celebrate our Savior and King.

Jesus said, "He who has an ear, let him hear what the Spirit says to the churches" (Rev 3:6). But can we hear the Spirit of God while our hearts are filled with the music of the world?

We, as the Lord's people called to a lifestyle of praise and thanksgiving, should not be naïve to the spiritual danger of yielding our minds to a sound that exhibits enmity toward God by its friendship with the world (cf. Js 4:4).

The prophet Isaiah spoke of how cultural harlotry is promoted through music:

> "Take a harp, go about the city, you forgotten
> harlot; make sweet melody, sing many songs,
> that you may be remembered" (23:16).

The songs of the harlot call to remembrance the pleasures of sin, and to receive her music is to be stirred by her spirit. Each of us can choose to listen or to not listen, but none of us can choose to escape the consequences of willfully absorbing the spirit of an unbelieving world.

A Christian who feels a need to enjoy the world's music does not have a developed understanding of the joy of making music to the Father through Jesus. Wherever you are, on a hiking trail or a hospital bed, a lakeside park or a prison cell, you can be "filled with the Spirit" by rejoicing with "psalms and hymns and spiritual songs, singing and making melody in your heart to the Lord" (Eph 5:18-19).

But can any of us truly glorify the Lord while our hearts are filled with the songs of this age?

Isaiah warns us through the Spirit against music that

stimulates ungodly thinking and conduct:

> "The harp and the strings, the tambourine and the flute, and wine are in their feasts; but they do not regard the work of the Lord, nor consider the operation of His hands" (5:12).

A musical experience that does not exalt "the work of the Lord" has no legitimate place in the creation of God. The Scripture commands "all the earth" to "break forth in song, rejoice, and sing praises" (Ps 98:4), but the voice of the world refuses to praise and darkens the mind through music that suppresses the knowledge of God.

If your life has been dry and unfruitful, you may need to assess your level of involvement with the world. Are you where you want to be spiritually? None of us are, but one thing we can do is put away the things that compromise us. The power of God works through faith, and "all things are possible" to those who believe without doubting. If you are eager for the power of God to move mountains in your life, you will need to embrace the Scriptures that instruct us to drive away doubt and worldliness by filling our hearts with continuous songs of praise.

The Scripture exhorts us to associate the meaning of life with praise, and to invest every moment with eternal value and with resurrection power by joyfully singing to God. As David vowed:

> "I will sing to the Lord as long as I live; I will

sing praise to my God while I have my being" (Ps 104:33).

For David, the value of each moment was its opportunity for bringing glory to God with songs of praise. And if we
expect to triumph through God as David did, we will sing as
David sang. Not because singing itself has magical value, but
simply because God has ordained song as a primary expression
of the worship through which union with the Creator is experienced.

Because song is so fundamental to the spiritual act of
worship for the glory of God and the good of man, the god of
this world exploits the mental impulse of song to celebrate re-
bellion, unbelief, and death. If the allurement of worldly music
has been a snare for you, you can deaden its influence by aggressively filling your heart with songs of joyful praise.
"Whoever offers praise glorifies Me" (Ps 50:23), and as you
cultivate in your mind a habitual pattern of spontaneous song
you will experience the power of the Spirit in ways you had not
imagined.

Songs of joy express the faith by which all things are
possible, as David wrote in a psalm for "the Chief Musician"
when "the Lord delivered him from the hand of all his enemies":

"For by You I can run against a troop, by my
God I can leap over a wall" (Ps 18:29).

When walls of opposition surround you, leap into your

day with songs of praise and sing with passion in the night:

"(I)n the night His song shall be with me—a prayer to
the God of my life" (Ps 42:8).

By songs of praise we lay hold on His strength and
confess our confidence in His mercy:

"I will sing of Your power; yes, I will sing
aloud of Your mercy in the morning...To You,
O my strength, I will sing praises; for God is
my defense, my God of mercy" (Ps 59:16-17).

The Bible shows how the people of God recorded His
exploits in songs to be learned and handed down, as when the
Lord provided Israel with water at a place they called Beer
("Well"):

"Then Israel sang this song: "Spring up, O
well! All of you sing to it—the well the leaders
sank, dug by the nation's nobles, by the law-
giver, with their staves"" (Num 21:17-18).

There are many examples of this in Biblical history, but
each of us can devise our own songs to celebrate the beauty and
the exploits of the Lord that we ourselves have witnessed:

"Come and hear, all you who fear God, and I
will declare what He has done for my soul. I

99

cried to Him with my mouth, and He was ex-
tolled with my tongue" (Ps 66:16-17).

"Sing to Him a new song; play skillfully with a
shout of joy" (Ps 33:3).

"I will sing to the Lord, because He has dealt
bountifully with me" (Ps 13:6).

Each one of us is authorized to offer songs that com-
memorate how the Lord "has dealt bountifully with me," and
by filling our hearts with creative songs we "worship God in
the Spirit" with sacrifices of delightful fragrance:

"May my meditation be sweet to Him; I will be
glad in the Lord" (Ps 104:34).

"I will praise the name of God with a song, and
will magnify Him with thanksgiving. This also
shall please the Lord" (Ps 69:30-31).

When you feel the urge to do something good and
pleasant, you can break out in song to God:

"For it is good to sing praises to our God" (Ps 147:1).

"Sing praises to His name, for it is pleasant" (Ps 135:3).

Does your life seem dull? Are you trapped in an ugly

circumstance, surrounded by boredom with no end in sight? You can beautify every moment and make it last forever by investing the moment with praise.

The Scripture tells us "the eyes of the Lord run to and fro throughout the whole earth, to show Himself strong on behalf of those whose heart is loyal to Him" (2Chron 16:9). Do you have cares that you are helpless to do anything about? A son or a daughter in the military? A runaway child whose whereabouts you do not know? The Scripture guarantees the Lord's involvement as you keep your heart loyal to Him, and there is no better way to fix your heart on God than to joyfully sing His praise. By worshipping Him with songs of thanksgiving you can know with joyful certainty that wherever on earth you have a care, the eye of the Lord is there to show Himself strong on your behalf.

Do not underestimate the reach of His power or the beauty of His mercy. Without leaving other things undone, cast all your cares on Him by "singing and making melody in your heart to the Lord." By offering songs of joyful worship you have put your cares into the hand of the living God, and what better place could you possibly put them?

The Scriptures so abundantly emphasize the beauty of song in the worship of God and the quality of life:

"Sing to Him, sing psalms to Him; talk of all His wondrous works" (1Chron 16:9).

"Sing out the honor of His name" (Ps 66:2).

"Shout joyfully before the Lord, the King" (Ps 98:6).

"Sing to the Lord a new song, and His praise from the ends of the earth" (Isa 42:10).

"We will sing and praise Your power" (Ps 21:13).

By rejoicing in His power we experience His power, as David sang "when he fled from Saul into the cave":

"I will cry out to God Most High, to God who performs all things for me...I will sing and give praise" (Ps 57:2,7).

In a time of absolute helplessness you can boldly say, "The Lord will perform all things for me while I sing and give praise."

We should never forget the example of Jehoshaphat when the kingdom of Judah faced impossible odds. The Scripture records how the king "appointed those who should sing to the Lord...as they went out before the army" (2Chron 20:21). Having done all that he could (he sent out the fighters), Jehoshaphat put the singers ahead of it all, and "when they began to sing and to praise, the Lord set ambushes against [the opposition]; and they were defeated" (vs 22).

Are you facing great opposition? Are you chained to addictions or restricted by a difficult circumstance? Do you feel dry in your spirit and insufficient for the work of ministry? The remedy for you is to sing to the Lord day and night. You do not need a long course on spiritual recovery. You do not need to climb a tall staircase of spiritual steps. You need to praise God.

The Scripture assures us:

> "God has gone up with a shout, the Lord with the sound of a trumpet. Sing praises to God, sing praises! Sing praises to our King, sing praises! For God is the King of all the earth" (Ps 47:5-7a).

If we truly believe that God is the King we will understand the value of praise, and the Scripture exhorts us to "sing praises with understanding" (Ps 47:7b). By faith we understand through the Scriptures that God has ordained praise "to silence the foe," and by constantly praising God you will turn the tables on every adversity in your life.

Do not let the stones take your blessing. Sing to the Lord with joyful songs and refuse to stop, knowing from the Scripture of truth and from historical example that the Lord will take control of your life if you come to Him boldly with songs of thanksgiving. By shouts and songs and "melody in your heart to the Lord" you will glorify Him with joyful faith as you march through your days in the triumph of praise.

A Word From the Authors...

Through your reading of *Kings of Praise* we trust you are convinced from Scripture (if you were not already) how a life of triumph is guaranteed by the power of God through faith expressed in joyful praise. If your faith had been limping you will now have learned that the remedy for unhealthy faith is to "break forth in song, rejoice, and sing praises."

May our God and Father, through Jesus Christ His Son, confirm to you the liberating and triumphant power of this knowledge as you come to Him boldly for the help you need. We hope that your joyfulness in the faith will also spill over in your household and workplace and community, touching those who need a living example of the fragrance of Christ for spurring them also to "taste and see that the Lord is good."

We thank you for reading this book, and we salute you in the love of Christ as you march through your day with songs of Jesus in your heart and shouts of glory on your lips.

A Word From the Publisher...

For other books and publications by J. Patrick Griffin, Jr., visit us at **www.MaryEllenGroup.com.**

Kings of Praise has shown the dynamic between constant praise and boldness of faith for a life of triumph in our Lord Jesus Christ. In a companion book, *Priests of Power*, Patrick and Carlos show from Scripture how a lifestyle of good works, accompanied by constant praise, brings to full maturity the faith by which "all things are possible."